Spiritual Giftedness

Empowering the Twenty-First
Century Church

Doug Hamilton

SUNSET
INSTITUTE PRESS
3710 34th Street • Lubbock, Texas • 79410
800-687-2121 • www.extensionschool.com

CONTENTS

Introduction 1
   I. How Can this Help My Congregation?. 5

  II. The Personal Benefits to Spiritual Giftedness. . . . 25

  III. Defining the Spiritual Gifts. 39

  IV. The Gift of Missions. 57

  V. The Gift of Evangelism. 73

  VI. The Gift of Confrontation. 87

  VII. The Gift of Teaching. 103

  VIII. The Gift of Nurturing. 121

  IX. The Gift of Encouragement. 139

  X. The Gift of Mercy Giving. 155

  XI. The Gift of Service. 169

  XII. The Gift of Management. 185

  XIII. The Gift of Charity/Benevolence. 203

APPENDIX. 219

Acknowledgments

As one will see from the contents within this publication, people are all gifted in many different ways. The success of any team is found in their ability to work together in respect to these strengths. The writing of this book is no different, for a diverse group of people participated from many ways. I wish to acknowledge them at this time.

Thank you Brian Dowler for your organizational skills and guidance. Thanks to Lisa Shaw, Anita Clark, Jennifer Marrs, Kristi McNeice, Wally and Grace Evans, Lou and Rayma Boccio, Jo Merrill and Jackie Probst for your detailed proof-reading skills. Each of you brought so much to the production of this writing.

I also express deep gratitude for the assistance of Charles Brown, Lindy and Carol Presson, Isabelle Heath, Natalie Curtis and Truitt Adair. I appreciate your feedback and encouragement as it was coming together. Thank you Seth Deitch and Richard Clark for donating your technological skills. A special thanks to Samantha Deitch for her wonderful artistic skill in capturing each chapter in a picture.

Finally, thank you to my family. You have helped me understand spiritual giftedness on the greatest level. Being with you and watching your ministerial passions grow to where they are has been such a joy.

FORWARD

I met Doug Hamilton and his then young family in 1997 when he began his ministry studies at Sunset. It was apparent very early that Doug was a gifted personal evangelist and public speaker who could "think on his feet." No wonder, since before coming to Sunset Doug had made a good living as a door to door salesman, selling, of all things, caskets and funeral plots to people who before he knocked on their door, felt absolutely no need for either. On an evangelistic "door knocking" campaign with him early in his times at Sunset, his gift became apparent when he set up more Bible studies than all the others combined. In those early years as a student Doug not only demonstrated the positive side of his gift of evangelism, but also some of the "signs of immaturity." He was excellent in academics, with a GPA above 95%. However, some of his teachers observed that he tended to come across as intimidating, over-confident, sometimes offensive and inconsiderate of others. Some feared that his effectiveness as a congregational minister would be limited by some of these weaknesses and that he would struggle to get along with people, especially his leaders.

Through the years God has enabled Doug to grow in his giftedness and deal with many of his earlier immaturities. He has grown in humility and consideration of others' feelings and has learned to be a good listener. He has grown from a "flaming Evangelist" into a broader spectrum of giftedness. I'm convinced that at least part of his successful journey of growth and development in a more balanced ministry is because of his study of Biblical giftedness. Doug has been exploring the positives and negatives of the ten spiritual passions or gifts for many years. He has conducted dozens of giftedness seminars across America and in a number of foreign countries. He has shared his research with me through the years and I have found it helpful in giftedness seminars I have conducted. The practical material in this book has grown out of his personal journey of faith and out of the journeys of many people he has helped to deploy their gifts effectively. The Biblical content was developed out of a deep study of God's inspired word. Doug has continued to grow as an accomplished Biblical scholar and a very good writer.

Truitt Adair, President
Sunset International Bible Institute

Doug is available to hold Spiritual Giftedness Seminars in your congregation. You can contact him at:

Camp Hill Church of Christ
3042 Cumberland Blvd.
Camp Hill, PA. 17011
(717) 737-5587

Introduction

There have been thousands of books written by Christians about Christian living. Some have focused on personal growth, some on evangelism, and some on various self-help topics. Yet with all the attempts to better serve Christ, the church in America has been consistently shrinking.

In February 2009, Bobby Ross Jr. published an article in the *Christian Chronicle* titled "Church in America Marked By Decline". He reported of the 12,629 a cappella Churches of Christ, comprised of 1,578,281 adherents nationwide, attendance over a six-year period dropped more than 78,000 members and 526 congregations. These are startling statistics and must be addressed.

This drop in attendance is not just among the Churches of Christ, but across the board for all Christian religious groups in the U.S. According to an October 17, 2014 article released from the Barna group, the churches in America are in grave trouble. The article is titled, "Unchurched America: They pray, own Bibles and are 'spiritual', but nearly half see no value in attending church." He revealed a truth that we may have already known. Barna concluded, "If churches hope to grow by discipling new believers, we must improve our ability to attract those who are intentionally avoiding a connection with the church."

Countless theories have been put forth to explain the decrease, including a change in the culture from church to "unchurched." Plans have been enacted, but many congregations continue to wane. Perhaps there is a simpler solution to the problem. According to a 1996 publication by Christian Schwartz, *Natural Church Development,* one of the primary reasons for the atrophied attendance among churches worldwide is that congregations do not engage members in their Spiritual Gifts. I am persuaded Schwartz was on track, for when people fail to incorporate their natural strengths within an organization, there is a tendency for that body to atrophy.

The apostle John said in 1 John 1:4 that it is God's intention for our "joy to be full." Jesus wants the Christian walk to be filled with joy, for that is what keeps one going through the turbulent times. There is no greater joy for a person than finding Christ and discovering their purpose within the local church body.

What I have witnessed over the past two decades of ministry work is that prospects often fail to convert to Christ because they cannot envision the greater picture; they do not know what their Spiritual Gifts are and how they might fit into the scheme of the church. Another observation is that when people do convert to Christ, they often do not stay faithful. This is not because they did not love the Lord, but because they failed to find their niche within the various works of the church family. If a person does not see where he or she fits within the mission of the church, he or she tends to not stay within the body.

What if Christians were able to see their potential within the church family from the very beginning? What if they were able to incorporate themselves into the church body in a way which would provide maximum personal joy? Would more come to Christ? Would more stay faithful in Christ? I am persuaded this is true and the accounts revealed in this book confirm it.

That is the aim of this publication—to empower the saints in their giftedness so that *their joy may be full*. We all have unique DNA (*deoxyribonucleic acid*) which individualizes each of us in the biological world. We can undergo testing at one of many genetic institutes to research what our biological weaknesses and strengths are, resulting in a more meaningful life. In like manner, we all have a nonphysical DNA (*Divine Natural Ability*) which sets us apart from others in the spiritual world. What might provide joy to one may not have the same effect on another. In this book you will be able to administrate your own *spiritual DNA* Test to discover how to find the peace, joy, and happiness that God wants in your life. There are ten ministerial passions which we will discuss in greater detail in chapter 3. By being able to identify these gifts, the spiritual DNA (*Divine Natural Ability* will become evident.

Throughout the writing, there will be many true life accounts to illustrate application. Some of the names may be changed to protect the innocent and the guilty. All scripture references will be from the New American Standard Updated Edition unless otherwise noted.

I pray that what is covered in the pages to come will bless you in a way that results in great spiritual growth, stronger relationships within the church family, and an active spiritual life, bringing you even closer to the throne seat of God. Thank you for joining me on this adventure.

Let us begin!

Chapter One

How Can This Help My Congregation?

Throughout this writing I will use the term *gift-oriented*. I do so in order to manage the perspective by which you should view the material. To be gift-oriented is to see yourself and others in a new perspective, not through the physical world, but through the spiritual. It is a mindset which allows us to look at others through a spiritual perspective, leading to a completely different outcome in our perception of one another and our work within the church.

Let us begin answering the question: "How can this help my congregation?" There are five perspectives of the church for the Christian to keep in mind when discussing gift-orientations. I refer to them as the five **E**'s of the functional church:

1) Evangelizing
2) Evaluating
3) Educating
4) Encouraging
5) Equipping

It is these five perspectives through which Spiritual Giftedness can empower the twenty-first century church. When the members of a congregation communally place these areas of ministry on a gift-oriented backdrop, then great results will follow.

1) Evangelizing

We are told to take the gospel to the entire world (Matthew 28:19; Mark 16:15), including our neighborhoods and homes. When we ask people to commit to Christ for the rest of their lives, the stakes are high. Jesus wants us to "calculate the cost" (Luke 14:28) in every major decision. There are two primary factors which people consider when making the big decisions of life; they are the fear of loss and the availability of gain. When someone comes to Jesus, it is imperative for them to realize that they are replacing a future in hell with one in heaven.

To illustrate this point, I would like to reference, in a metaphorical sense, a common tool we use in navigation in the modern age called Global Positioning System (GPS). In the spiritual realm we have a GPS (God Positional Salvation). It uses love of heaven and fear of hell as points of reference. When we lose this two-fold perspective of the gospel decision, our spiritual GPS does not give accurate readings. This results in making less informed decisions. When a potential convert is aware of their spiritual passion, it can actually be a guide to lead him to Christ.

I am persuaded the deeply held desires of an individual are soul deep and present before conversion. When we are baptized into the possession of the Father, Son and the Holy Spirit, our heart, soul, and mind are now claimed for the work of the kingdom. If we loved pizza prior to conversion, does that change after? Of course not! We make spiritual adjustments like avoidance of gluttony, but we still love pizza! That part of us really does not change.

In the same way, our spiritual passions prior to conversion are not simply set aside when we choose to serve the Lord. If someone enjoyed helping others prior to entering covenant with Christ, does that mean they no longer enjoy helping others after? If a person enjoyed being the bearer of good news prior to conversion, does that mean they do not enjoy sharing good news after? Certainly not!

The key here is to understand that our gift-orientation does not change with our conversion to Christ. Rather it becomes magnified towards purposeful work in Christ. This is significant because while we may have previously used our gifts for sinful, personal gain, we now have the ability to use them to grow the kingdom. One of the functions of the leadership within the congregation is to recognize what our gifts are and how best they can be used for the work of the kingdom.

The Seeking Servant/Teacher

While holding a Spiritual Giftedness seminar in the Midwest, I met a young man named Paul. He had family in the local congregation, but had not yet committed to Jesus. He decided to attend the meeting nonetheless just to make the relatives happy. While there, he witnessed many Christians taking the written Spiritual Giftedness exam, then talking about and sharing their strengths and weaknesses with each other. He asked if he could take the test, and I said that it was fine. He tested extremely high in Teacher and Servant. When he asked what it meant, I told him that his passions were with deep study and helping people.

With that knowledge, I issued an evangelistic challenge to him. First, take one book of the Bible and study it as much as possible over the next thirty days. He was to glean as much information as he could from it. Secondly, he was to help the members of the church as much as allowable over the same period of time. He was to be the best Servant possible. I said, "If after thirty days you are not happy about what you find, then move on with a clear conscience, knowing that you attempted to see things through the eyes of God."

About three months later, I received an email from Paul. He told me that he did as we discussed for thirty days and really liked it. He decided to do it for another month, resulting in more enjoyment. He repeated it for another month and further ignited his passion for God. He concluded his email by saying he was baptized into Jesus that evening! Paul had seen a purpose in his life and experienced some of the joy he could have as a Christian. Yes, he knew from the past about hell and repentance. Now his understanding was from the practical perspective of serving Jesus from the moment he came up out of the water.

Being Gift-Oriented Does Make A Difference.

You can effectively use Spiritual Giftedness to lead others to Christ by showing them the value that God has already placed in them. There have been numerous times that individuals have made the decision to convert, founded upon the possibilities open to them for service to God. The overall growth and development of the congregation is dependent upon the leadership's ability to discover, develop, and interconnect each member's gifts into reliable service for Jesus.

Gifts Around the World

While holding some meetings in Kakinada, India in 2003, I noticed the power of Spiritual Giftedness concerning evangelism was applicable, even in a foreign country. During a two-day meeting for equipping the saints at the Kakinada Church of Christ, we kept this strategy in mind. I spoke prior with the minister of the congregation and asked if we could use the material for evangelism as well as equipping. Naturally, being extremely passionate about evangelism, he readily agreed. Every lesson taught was from a dual perspective.

At the end of the first day, there were seven souls baptized into Christ. At the end of the second day, another eight were added. With the minister translating the lessons into their native tongue, many of the new converts could see where they would fit into the church family before converting. They had a communal vision of belonging, adding a deeper meaning for their potential new life in Christ. Later in the week, at another seminar of the same topic, six more souls were added to Christ. Before the mission was over, more than two-hundred had converted to Jesus.

When the lost see the grace of Jesus and also the joy they can experience in serving Him, they are more capable of then weighing both the costs and the benefits. Sharing the joy of Spiritual Giftedness is a needed, yet often overlooked, tool for evangelism. A congregation is only as sound as the empowered members that comprise it. This is essential in helping the congregation grow.

2) Evaluating

Evaluating people is something we do as individuals each and every day. We interact with others and observe their speech, body language, and responses to inquiry. This is par for the course in both everyday life and in being a servant of the Lord. There is a need to better understand people both in and outside the church family. When you know that someone is gifted in one area and weak in another, then you can better adjust your interactions to handle issues that arise. Your treatment of matters with that person will be much better in the end.

The Failed Food Bank

There was a congregation that had a failing food bank ministry. It wasn't because they weren't bringing in enough food through donations, but rather the food was growing old sitting on the shelves. I held a seminar about two weeks after they ended the ministry. They were extremely high in Giving (15%) and low on Mercy Giving (3%). Basically put, they had a deep desire to donate groceries, but had poor connections to give the food away.

The Mercy Givers of a congregation usually number about 17%. They serve as magnets for forgotten people, bringing the hurting and needy to the church family. The congregation was unable to naturally make the connection to the hurting souls who needed the food. With that analysis of the congregation's Spiritual Giftedness, the members could more effectively deal with that type of ministry. Through classes on how to reach out to the hurting of the community, they adjusted their approach.

Evaluation is the Key

Countless times we have judged books by their covers without ever having read a page. People's motivations must be taken into consideration when interacting on a daily basis. One with the ministerial passion of the Mercy Giver will view a situation differently than a Teacher. The Encourager is very different than the Missionary. The Evangelist holds a different perspective than the Administrator. When each ministerial passion is taken into consideration, unity is more likely to occur.

Lonely Hearts

Years ago, I was holding a number of these Spiritual Giftedness seminars in Pennsylvania. My goal was primarily to meet some of the many church members in my area. During that time, I went on a mountain hike with some fellow Christians from the classes. One of our single female members expressed sadness that there was not a prospective spouse for her in the church. She was thinking of moving away to another location partially for that reason.

I told her about a man from another small-group Bible study who appeared to be a good match for her. He was opposite in gift-orientation, and they tend to attract in marriage. The next day we arranged for that brother to go on another hike which included her. They hit it off with great admiration for one another. Within six months they were married and remain in that union today. She saw qualities in him and vice-versa that really helped them to evaluate one another for an important, life-changing decision like marriage.

This book will better help you understand the differences between Spiritual Gifts and the relative compatibility with others. In a later chapter I show you how various gifts relate to personality types and how to avoid pairing too many of one type based on a well-defined goal.

The Best Tool to Evaluate

Often when meeting couples with marriage difficulties, I will give them a Spiritual Giftedness exam and take them through the course. This aids me in identifying potential sources of conflict by focusing on areas of weakness. Sometimes a couple does not see the uniqueness of their spouse and how they really complement one another. By evaluating their gift-orientations, things seem to go smoother because people are more understanding of each other. When a wife sees the value of a husband through the eyes of God, and when he sees his wife's value in the same way, then harmony will more than likely result.

Pretending that everyone is the same does not serve the church family well and usually leads to trouble. While we may all share the same God, the same Jesus, and follow a common doctrine, it does not eliminate the unique characteristics of each individual. If we would simply calculate Spiritual Giftedness into the equation, then many of our problems would not get out of hand. There would be fewer difficulties and the ones that would arise would be more readily extinguished.

The Angry Servant

Another way I like to use this information is in conflict resolution. I once received a call from a sister informing me that there would be a family calling for benevolence. Later that day, they called, and we discussed their pressing need. Since my passion is Evangelist/Teacher, I naturally wanted to meet the family for the purpose of opening the door for possible conversion to Christ. My plan was to meet them, minister to their need, and find what spiritual needs they might have. They said, "We just want you to send the money to this address and not have anyone call or meet with us." To me, this was not a good use of church funds, for it was not being a wise steward of God's blessings. Needless to say, we did not help them.

When the sister from the church found out, she was very angry with me. She expressed the need to give first and without question when there is a need. Having met with her many times in the past, I determined her to be Servant/Mercy Giver/Giver. I could have tried to argue the point with her from a right/wrong perspective, but I chose the Spiritual Gifts route.

I explained that she viewed the incident from a different standpoint, the Giving, Merciful, Helper perspective. She readily agreed it was how she felt. I asked her how she would have reasoned had they told her, "We want you to just have a Bible study, no giving, no hospitality, no acts of kindness, no mercy in anyway, just the Bible lesson!" She responded that it would be ridiculous to her. I explained that I am gifted as Evangelist/ Teacher. Further explaining their intention, I was not willing to agree to their "Just give me the money!" terms. Is that any different? We were able to see the situation from the other's perspective and, thirteen years later, are still good friends.

In the above example, we can see a difference in perspectives, but with the same resulting logic. People with different gifts will see things contrarily, depending on the level of emotion that might be built into the scenario. Patience is important when dealing with each person and respect for his or her gifts is essential.

3) Educating

Education is of obvious importance both to being a Christian and also to life in general. Our decision-making capabilities are directly tied to our education. Likewise, how we process information will depend to some degree on how well we are educated, both spiritually and academically.

What is a typical strategy in choosing education? Often we plan to have instruction in the areas we want instead of those we actually need. 1 Timothy 4:16 states, *"Pay close attention to yourself and to your teaching..."* It would be appropriate for everyone to take heed of these words when it comes to application of the *gift-oriented* curriculum.

The Gift-Oriented Education

The strategy is to *labor in the strengths* and, at the same time, *educate in the weaknesses*. It is natural for people to want to stick only with what comes naturally. It is through education in the areas of weaknesses that a congregation will be able to change for the better.

The Bible says in Hosea 4:6, *"...My people are destroyed for lack of knowledge..."* In the same manner, a people will also perish due to lack of knowledge of Spiritual Gifts. Hosea was speaking in the context of knowledge as it pertains to the children of Israel being unwilling to understand God's plan. The sentiment is resoundingly clear in terms of the wisdom behind understanding Spiritual Gifts.

Gift-Oriented Curriculum

While holding the Spiritual Giftedness seminar in New England, the congregation was tested and results were tabulated. They came out extremely high in Servant, Giver, and Mercy Giver, but extremely low in Teacher, Prophet, and Evangelist. Like most congregations, they were active in their strengths, while ignoring the future potential of their weaknesses. When the seminar was complete, I provided a feedback report.

Since this group was weak in Prophet, Teacher, and Evangelist, I advised them to have many series of lessons on those subjects. The education committee developed studies on the price of sin, as well as hermeneutics and evangelism. When a special events speaker would come, they requested not the lessons they wanted to hear, but what they needed to hear.

When a congregation does this on a regular basis, they mix a blend of new information into their present labors. The result will be a more gift-oriented, balanced congregation that is able to do all things well instead of a few things great. Do they maintain their same passions? Yes! Are they better able to use all of them for the kingdom? Yes!

The true challenge for all congregations is maintaining stamina in the areas where they are weakest. This comes down to leadership being able to apply the wisdom that they have been given, ensuring that all gifts are equally addressed.

Gift-Focused Preachers

Athens International Bible Institute (AIBI) in Greece uses this Spiritual Giftedness series in their curriculum. Why? It is because this allows the students to have a better understanding of one another, as well as the congregations they will be working with in the future. Why do some preachers feel stronger about the gospel than others? Why do some ministers feel stronger about visiting the sick and the poor more than others? Why do some preachers seem like they are always compiling plans and lessons while others do not? I am persuaded this is in large part due to the many differences in the giftedness of individuals.

Not all great speakers are, nor should be, preachers. Some great preachers are sorely lacking in the complementary gifts, often without even knowing it. I will cover this in the analyses of each gift's general strengths and weaknesses throughout the book.

Gift-Balanced Lessons

I have a confession to make about preaching. I tend to screen my sermons through a Spiritual Giftedness filter before speaking. When speaking, I am careful not to give too many Evangelist-flavored sermons. This is a very common mistake among preachers and leads to all sorts of trouble. Instead, I pay close attention to the other Spiritual Gifts which make up the congregation.

Some preachers have a tendency to speak only the Servant/Mercy Giver types of sermons; others will put the hammer down with hell-fire and brimstone Prophet sermons. Many preachers who are of the Teacher passion will tend to go into too much detail. These lessons can quickly grow old if preachers fail to use a variety. Would it not be better to feed the entire congregation instead of just a few?

The same goes for encouraging others to teach, even if their Spiritual Giftedness is not Teaching. One of our members tested extremely low in Teacher and extremely high in Encourager. When I asked him if he wanted to teach a Bible study, he initially said "No." When I told him the class was titled "How to Encourage Others", he said "Yes! You did not say it was about that!" His response was such because he already had the passion of the Encourager and spoke it fluently. Balancing the church curriculum in consideration of Spiritual Giftedness is a good thing.

4) Encouraging

The word *encourage* means "to put courage in" another person. We are told in the scriptures to be an encouragement to one another. 1Thessalonians 5:11 says, "Therefore encourage one another and build up one another..." That is not always so easy when dealing with the different passions of the church, but to the gift-oriented individual it becomes much easier.

Back in the 1990s, I made my first mission trip overseas, with the country of choice being Romania. Up until that point, I had never been to an area of the world where English was not the primary language. After a week, we went to the bank to exchange some additional funds, and it was a rather strange experience. I was among a large group of Romanians, hearing the conversations going on around me and not understanding what was being said. It was rather lonely to be there standing in line. Then, from across the room, I heard in a Texas accent, "I would like to swap some of these US dollars into Romanian Lei." Out of the many dozens of voices I heard, there was one that instantly encouraged me, for it was my mother tongue. Needless to say, we had a wonderful conversation with each other about our visit to the country.

When we fail to speak another person's Spiritual Gift language, we end up being put into a position of not being able to effectively encourage them. If we can figure out their foremost language (either Servant, Administration, Shepherd, Missions, or whatever else it might be), then our ability to encourage them drastically improves.

The Comforted Wounded

Many years ago, there was an elderly woman from our congregation who hosted a Bible study for more than a decade. Her top ministerial passions were obvious even before being tested: Encourager/Servant/Giver. Like most retired individuals her age, she suffered from health problems. Despite those issues, she usually answered the door with a bright smile, a kind phrase, and a warm hug.

One day she was far from well. She had recently suffered a bad bout of the flu and a torn retina in her right eye. To make matters worse, she also hurt her back in a fall while attempting to assist her husband. Coming to the door, she looked like death warmed over on a cold plate. Very exhausted, she grunted, "I am pretty tired and don't really think I could enjoy a study today."

I felt she could use some real encouragement, but the detailed Teacher/Evangelist lesson would not do the trick. I made sure to focus on her spiritual language. That day, she heard a lesson about how we need to take the time to encourage each other with our acts of service and redistribution of our blessings. Almost immediately, she began to light up when she heard her natural, fluent ministerial tongue. By the time it was over, she smacked the table with her little fist, with a smile on her face and joy in her heart, saying,

"You preach it Doug!" Before leaving, she hugged me and said, "Thank you! I am so happy we had the lesson today!"

We Understand Other People's Languages

Time and time again, I have run into tough situations which would have turned out much better if only those involved would have taken the time to understand Spiritual Giftedness. If we attempt to communicate to the Shepherd using the Prophet's language, very little will be accomplished. The Evangelist does not fluently speak the Servant's language. I have witnessed division and failure occur numerous times simply because of a breakdown in communication along these lines.

The Misunderstood Mercy Giver

Sally was a young mother who found out she was pregnant with her second child. A couple of hours before, she discovered that her husband of five years was leaving her for another woman. Needless to say she was devastated to the point of hospitalization for the depression. Life for her as a single and expecting parent would require some obvious changes.

One of her difficulties was that she worked in a nursing home nearly twenty-five miles away. With the cold, Midwestern winter fast approaching, her church family thought it would be best for her to take a job in her local community. Some brothers from the congregation were able to pull some strings and get Sally a job interview at a local meat packing plant. It would be closer to town, pay much more, and give her some safety from the cold winter.

She went to the job interview, and it went well. The brethren knew from inside sources that she was going to be offered the job. The church was in great spirits, having come to her aid. The problem arose, however, when she turned down their offer for seemingly no good reason. The church members were a bit upset, having put forth a good effort to assist her.

A few months later, Sally happened to be tested in Spiritual Giftedness. She came back with the highest possible score in

Mercy Giver. It was then that her church family finally understood why she could not take the job. As she said, "You cannot show mercy to a ten-pound pork loin roast, but only to hurting people." Later, in reflection of the decision, Sally told the preacher, "If I could not minister to those lonely and forgotten residents of the nursing home, I would have never made it." Understanding her Spiritual Giftedness perspective, the congregation was then better able to minister to her spiritually and emotionally.

5) Equipping

The final category concerns the equipping of the saints. Ephesians 4:12 teaches that the Bible is profitable "for the equipping of the saints for the work of service, to the building up of the body of Christ…" Congregations throughout the world are filled with souls longing to be used in service to Jesus. They must be empowered!

The Rejuvenated Retiree

Juanice always wanted to be a missionary. She grew up in the church meeting with visiting missionaries; she always kept up with their adventures through the mission reports. She trained like a missionary and married a preacher with intentions of going to a mission field. Some life changes occurred, some plans fell through, and her mission dream was put on hold. For the next few decades, she worked domestically and raised her children. Throughout that time she suffered terrible, life-threatening illnesses. All the while, she held onto the hope of someday going to a foreign mission field.

Juanice was in her late fifties when I met her. She was a semi-retired worker at the local newspaper. She was one of my supporters for a mission trip to Romania. Upon receiving my report after my return, she left an emotionally filled five-minute phone message about how much she enjoyed it and wished she could have been there with us. I said to myself, "This lady is one flaming

Missionary." (The obvious presence of a ministerial passion.)

Ironically it was her home congregation which became my first full-time ministry work upon graduation from school. At the end of my first year, I announced there was another mission scheduled to Romania and that if anyone had an interest to let me know. Following the service, there was Juanice, frail from poor health, but joyous with hope. She said, "I already have the money saved up for the ticket and would love to go." Her passion was great – how could I resist her enthusiasm?

When some of the church family expressed concern over her health, I explained to them about her deep passion of Missions. They were satisfied with the explanation. She was adamant about making the trip, and I could not wait to see what she would do for the Romanians. All the plans were made. She would teach a ladies class and assist in the ministry for babies dying of AIDS at the Ploiesti hospital.

About two months before we were scheduled to depart, Juanice's husband had a stroke. With great sadness, some of the members of the church family advised her to scrap her plans to go. When she went to her husband, who had been rejoicing with her for the upcoming mission, he insisted that she go. He said he could have a family member stay with him while she went. He knew from her health issues that it might be the last time she may ever be able to go.

She made that trip to Romania, held the dying orphans and taught several classes to the women of the church. They loved her, and she loved them. Her Missionary heart had experienced a great moment in her life.

Juanice wrote six articles about the trip for the local newspaper for which she was employed. She communicated such passion in her stories of the suffering children of Ploiesti that it rallied the community throughout the course of the next year. Another trip was planned—large amounts of money raised, hospital equipment gathered, and new volunteers, some from outside the church family, recruited.

Juanice would not make that mission trip, for she had another bout with cancer, one which took her to the mission field of heaven. At her funeral, in the head panel of the casket, there was a picture of her sitting in the classroom in Romania. In the photograph she had the largest "Mission-Accomplished" smile on her face. The family told me at the funeral that she was never so happy in her life than when in Romania as a missionary. She had been fully equipped and empowered for her passion in life.

We Must Be Properly Equipped.

There can be no empowerment of an individual unless they are properly equipped. The problem typically comes up when we attempt to equip another in what is not their passion. In 1 Samuel 17:38-40, we find the account of David and Goliath. David was about to go out on the field to face the giant when King Saul offered him his royal armor. David *"tried to walk"*, but could not, because he was improperly equipped. *"So David said to Saul, 'I cannot go with these, for I have not tested them.' And David took them off."* The young shepherd boy was a fighter with slings and stones, not with the armor of a king. It certainly would have been a different outcome had he accepted being burdened with someone else's view of equipping.

Service in the church is similar. If we attempt to equip a Mercy Giver with the passion of the Evangelist, failure is prone to occur. If we place the passion of the Servant upon the heart of the Teacher, burnout will likely result.

The Equipped Addict

William grew up in the church and became a Christian at a young age. As time went on, like many kids in their teenage years, he hung out with the wrong people at the wrong time and ended up using drugs. This carried on into his early adult years and eventually began to destroy his life. After being kicked out of two brotherhood schools, many apartments, rehabs and people's lives, he finally ended up back home.

After working with him for a number of months, I noticed that he was extremely gifted in Teaching, for he paid attention to the finer details. As his mind was healing from the drugs, he reached another level in his recovery. I asked him if he would like to teach one of the home Bible studies on the Book of Galatians. He resisted, saying he did not know enough about it. I asked him to memorize the entire book and when it was complete, then he would be ready. He completed the memory work in only ten days!

In the next two months, he had another two books of the Bible memorized! It wasn't long until he was teaching our youth group and going on a foreign mission trip. In less than three years, he was attending a school of preaching and had already memorized many more books of the Bible. He was an excellent teacher and a wonderful example to addicts in recovery.

William knew his passion and pursued it. He was properly equipped, being able to envision what God had in store for him. It is in the equipping stage that Christians will be driven to *"mount up with wings like eagles"* (Isaiah 40:32) and soar to new heights in their Christian service in the kingdom.

Conclusion:

What would our local churches look like if we were *Gift-Oriented* in our mindset concerning the five **E**'s of church growth? Our **E**vangelizing, **E**valuating, **E**ducating, **E**ncouraging, and **E**quipping would be much more effective in the end. More members of the church would be motivated in their work in all aspects of their Christian lives.

Chapter Two

The Personal Benefits of Spiritual Giftedness

The Personal Benefits to Spiritual Giftedness

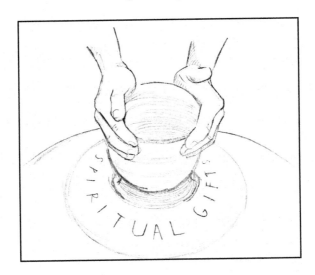

Throughout this course of study there will be hundreds of scripture references, however the primary passages are found in Romans 12, Ephesians 4, and 1 Peter 4. From these three sections of scripture, I will provide eight reasons why you should be Gift-Orientated in your mindset.

1) To Offer Oneself Up as a Living and Holy Sacrifice

Romans 12:1, *"I urge you therefore, brethren, by the mercies of God, to present your bodies a living and holy sacrifice, acceptable to God, {which is} your spiritual service of worship."*

Paul calls for us to present our lives as a sacrifice unto God. This passage is metaphorically referring to the burnt offering found in Leviticus 1. The fact that we are *"living"* sacrifices confirms that our Christian lives are an ongoing process. Numbers 28:3-8 speaks of a continual burnt offering. It was to be offered every morning and evening to commemorate Jewish devotion to God. We are also to continually offer ourselves daily for the service of God. As Paul said concerning his relationship with Christ in *1 Corinthians 15:31, "I die daily."*

In Ephesians 4:1 Paul further states, *"I, therefore, the prisoner of the Lord, entreat you to walk in a manner worthy of the calling with which you have been called…"* Christians are in a life-long relationship with their Savior Jesus. We are to *"walk in the Light as He Himself is in the Light"* (1 John 1:5), resulting in fellowship with the Creator of the universe (John 1:3). We are all called to serve God fully, but what happens when we fail to use our gifts for God? We become a spiritual zombie rather than saying, "Take me Lord for Your service!"

The Misdiagnosed Servant

Sarah was a kind-hearted elderly sister from a Northeast congregation whom I met more than a decade ago. She attended the Spiritual Giftedness Seminar at her local congregation over a three-day weekend and had taken the written examination. She also cross-referenced it with the four other confirmations (this is further explained in chapter three). On the last day of classes, she took me aside in the foyer and with tears in her eyes, she poured her heart out to me.

She said, "For the past four decades I have tried door-knocking campaigns for evangelism outreach, but never felt any joy in it. I am very high in Servant, but lowest in Evangelist. I was being someone whom I was not." Placing my hand on her shoulder, I replied, "Be who God made you to be and fit into the mission of your congregation as a Servant."

About two months later, I received a letter from Sarah. She told me how she started baking cookies and distributing them with a worship schedule attached to the bag. Sarah gladly went to the doors of the community and passed them out one house at a time. She said, "It took forty years, but I finally found my joy in Christ in evangelism."

2) To Not Be Conformed to This World

Romans 12:2, *"And do not be conformed to this world, but be transformed by the renewing of your mind, that you may prove what the will of God is, that which is good and acceptable and perfect."*

We are called not to conform, but to be transformed. To appreciate what Paul was teaching, it is necessary to look closely at a couple of the key words.

The first is *"conformed"*. It means *to fashion oneself* into the shape of another. Being middle action, it implies something that one does to self. In other words, we are the ones who have a decision to resist being fashioned into the pattern of the world. It is our own decision to fight against the natural tendencies of the world. I John 2:15 says to, *"Love not the world, neither the things that are in the world. If any man love the world, the love of the Father is not in him."*

The second word of focus which Paul used for *"transformed"* was *"metamorphoo"*. It is from which we derive the word *metamorphosis*, being similar to a caterpillar in a cocoon. The term is passive action, meaning something we allow to occur to us. The caterpillar has the decision to make and enter the cocoon, but God is the One who ultimately makes the change into the butterfly. The same applies to us. Here are two other places the word was used.

- Mark 9:2-3, *"And six days later, Jesus took with Him Peter and James and John, and brought them up to a high mountain by themselves. And He was transfigured before them; and His garments became radiant and exceedingly white, as no launderer on earth can whiten them."*
- 2 Corinthians. 3:18, *"But we all, with unveiled face beholding as in a mirror the glory of the Lord, are being transformed into the same image from glory to glory, just as from the Lord, the Spirit."*

To the non-conforming Christian there awaits a wonderful transformation by God. When we submit to the Spiritual Giftedness that Jesus has bestowed upon us. When we do, then we will be in the position of being transformed by Him. We surrender ourselves to be clay in the hands of God (Jeremiah 18:6) and He forms us into the vessel of His choice. The old Christian hymn written by Adelaide A. Pollard says it best.

> Have Thine own way, Lord! Have Thine own way!
> Thou art the Potter, I am the clay.
> Mold me and make me after Thy will,
> While I am waiting, yielded and still.

When we use the ministerial passions God has put in us, we are allowing Him to "transfigure" us into the image of His Son. In the end, if we refuse to use our Spiritual Gifts, then we may end up conforming to the world.

3) To Teach Personal Humility

Romans 12:3, *"For through the grace given to me I say to every man among you not to think more highly of himself than he ought to think; but to think so as to have sound judgment, as God has allotted to each a measure of faith."*

The number one problem that has plagued the harmony of congregations is our inability to maintain personal humility. We are to be as stated in Ephesians 4:2, *"...with all humility and gentleness, with patience, showing forbearance to one another in love..."* Spiritual Gifts allow us to recognize the personal value of others in the church family. When we observe that God has diversely invested His ministerial passions among the congregation, then humility will become second nature.

We are told in Philippians 2:3-4, *"Do nothing from selfishness or empty conceit, but with humility of mind let each of you regard one another as more important than himself; do not {merely} look out for your own personal interests, but also for the interests of others."* There is a natural yielding which takes place in the life of the one who utilizes their Spiritual Gift. He or she values what other saints from the congregation can offer and this results in humility.

<u>Personal Humility in Action</u>

When I was interviewed for my full-time preaching position at Camp Hill in 2002, we had an elderly, semi-retired preacher named Paul Cantrell. He held the full-time ministry position there in the 1970's and had returned to the area to be with his children and grandchildren. The congregation decided to hire him on a part-time basis, which can spell trouble for a new preacher coming in, setting up a possible power struggle.

Paul and his wife Mildred invited us to their home for a meal that Sunday afternoon. While there I saw his extensive, well-organized library and listened to him speak. I determined he was an Administrator/Teacher. Being highest in Evangelist and low in Administration, I am not comfortable sitting in an office and hammering out lessons. I am in my natural environment in people's homes for Bible studies. Here was my opportunity to rub elbows with an elderly man who could sharpen me in my weakness (Proverbs 27:17).

After preaching my evening sermon, Paul and I visited in the parking lot before my departure for the Baltimore airport. I confirmed to him, "If the congregation decides to hire me to work here, then I will look forward to learning from a man such as you. We will be able to accomplish much in our mission." I was humbling myself before Paul for what he brought to the mission in Christ in Camp Hill, for I saw his Spiritual Gifts very clearly.

I was hired and worked well with him. In fact, he became the father figure I never had. He kept the office hours, working on his teaching curriculum and planning years of classes for our congregation. I would hold most of the small-group, home Bible studies, make most of the hospital visits and go to the nursing homes. For nearly a decade I would meet Paul in his office and glean from the years of his Administrative experience. It was one of the saddest days in my life when I preached his funeral. I respected him for a hundred reasons, but the greatest reason was for his humility in Administration. He taught me more through his gifts than any book could have done.

4) To Add Value to Personal Ministry
Romans 12:4, *"For just as we have many members in one body and all the members do not have the same function..."*

Christians are to walk with Christ and share the hope of eternal life, but all Christians are not the same in their giftedness. 1 Corinthians 12:14-18 instructs, *"For the body is not one member, but many. If the foot should say, 'Because I am not a hand, I am not {a part} of the body,' it is not for this reason any the less {a part} of the body. And if the ear should say, 'Because I am not an eye, I am not {a part} of the body,' it is not for this reason any the less {a part} of the body. If the whole body were an eye, where would the hearing be? If the whole were hearing, where would the sense of smell be? But now God has placed the members, each one of them, in the body, just as He desired."*

The diversity of Spiritual Giftedness in a congregation allows each of the members to appreciate what they bring to the table. Various ministries require numerous individuals with many passions. A successful mission team is not made up of only Evangelists and Teachers - others bring their own passions with them as well. Administrators can assist well in planning; Encouragers can draw others in; Shepherds will bring about personal growth; Mercy Givers will comfort; Servants will complete important tasks. Everyone plays an important part in the vision.

Everyone Must Play a Part
There was a mission team of preacher students who went to a domestic mission field to *"turn the world upside down"* for Christ (Acts 17:6). They raised support and worked with the local

congregation. After about a year they disbanded and headed their separate ways. Why? This happened because they were all the same in their giftedness, which was Evangelist/Teacher. They would often overwhelm their prospects and overwork the congregation.

The first few months were okay, but after that time the others from the congregation would become "unavailable" when needed. They could not keep up with the missionaries. Even more complications arose because the missionaries did not take into consideration the Spiritual Gifts of the other members. In the end, there were very few converts and even fewer parishioners interested in continuing the work. This is called burnout.

5) To Teach Us the Oneness of the Body of Christ

Romans 12:5, *"... so we, who are many, are one body in Christ, and individually members one of another."*

Ephesians 4:3-5, *"...being diligent to preserve the unity of the Spirit in the bond of peace. {There is} one body and one Spirit, just as also you were called in one hope of your calling; one Lord, one faith, one baptism, one God and Father of all who is over all and through all and in all."*

There are seven points of unity for the Christian, one body, one Spirit, one hope, one Lord, one faith, one baptism and one God. He gave us gifts so that we would be unified in purpose, in spirit, and in vision. The employment of their Spiritual Gifts brings the best out of all the members. They are individually members one of another, causing them to work together for the common good. Together they are one, *"having a mind to work"* (Nehemiah 4:6).

Administrators in Action

When I hold the Spiritual Giftedness Seminar for a congregation, I make a report for the church family. It provides some guidance concerning their mission goals. In one Midwest congregation I met with the elders on a Sunday afternoon to give them the feedback. We tested more than 85% of the members and discovered they were extremely low on Administration. There were only four in the whole group, three of which were sisters in Christ. The elders, all whom tested low in that category, were suffering from a lack of planning. I suggested they go to the four members with a passion for Administration and task them with coming up with some solutions for congregationally employing their gifts. They took that advice.

Later that month I received a call from one of the elders, and he shared with me the marvelous idea that their four Administrators had submitted. They would have a large bulletin board with the congregation's vision listed across the top. Underneath they would have the ten Spiritual Gift categories with the various tasks needing assistance. The individual members, knowing their passions, would simply write their name next to the job.

Why didn't I come up with that great idea? It is because I am extremely low in that Administration. There is "Oneness" in the body of Christ and the Spiritual Gifts will always bring it about.

6) To Better Understand He Who Gives

Ephesians 4:7-10, *"But to each one of us grace was given according to the measure of Christ's gift. Therefore it says, 'When He ascended on high, He led captive a host of captives, and He gave gifts to men.' (Now this {expression,} 'He ascended,' what does it mean except that He also had descended into the lower parts of the earth? He who descended is Himself also He who ascended far above all the heavens, that He might fill all things.)"*

Christ has been graceful to each member of His church based on who He is. What does it imply when it said in verse 8, *"He gave gifts to men"*? This is a quote from Psalms 68:18, illustrating the reception of gifts to men. In order to give a gift, one must first possess the gift, otherwise it is the distribution of stolen property. Jesus gave all these gifts unto men because He already possessed all of them from the beginning. We see all of these passions exhibited in His life.

> Prophet: Matthew 7:29, *"... for He was teaching them as {one} having authority, and not as their scribes."*
> Service: Mark 10:45, *"For even the Son of Man did not come to be served, but to serve, and to give His life a ransom for many."*
> Teacher: Matthew 19:16, *"And behold, one came to Him and said, "Teacher, what good thing shall I do that I may obtain eternal life?"*
> Exhortation: 1 Corinthians 1:10, *"I exhort you, brethren, by the name of our Lord Jesus Christ..."*
> Giver: Acts 20:35, *"...He Himself said, 'It is more blessed to give than to receive.'"*
> Mercy Giver: 1 Timothy 1:2, *"Grace, mercy {and} peace from God the Father and Christ Jesus our Lord."*
> Leader: Matthew 23:10, *"And do not be called leaders; for One is your Leader, {that is,} Christ."*
> Shepherd: 1 Peter 5:4, *"And when the Chief Shepherd appears, you will receive the unfading crown of glory."*
> Evangelist: Matthew 9:35, **"***Jesus was going through all the cities and villages, teaching in their synagogues and proclaiming the gospel of the kingdom..."*
> Missionary: Mark 16:15, "And He said to them, "Go into all the world and preach the gospel to all creation."

When one with the Spiritual Gift of a Servant pours out his labors into others around him, we better understand Jesus. When the one with the Spiritual Gift of Evangelism fervently speaks his gospel message, we learn more about the Savior. When the one with the Spiritual Gift of Encouragement puts courage into the heart of the faint, we see our Lord in a new light. Through the exercise of the Spiritual Gifts, we better understand Jesus, the Giver of the gifts.

The Personal Benefits to Spiritual Giftedness

7) To Bring the Church to Her Fullness

Ephesians 4:11-13, *"And He gave some {as} apostles, and some {as} prophets, and some {as} evangelists, and some {as} pastors and teachers, for the equipping of the saints for the work of service, to the building up of the body of Christ; until we all attain to the unity of the faith, and of the knowledge of the Son of God, to a mature man, to the measure of the stature which belongs to the fullness of Christ."*

The Spiritual Gifts which God provides assists the church in functioning as a well-oiled machine. The congregations who use their gifts accordingly are fully equipped for service to the others around them. They are building one another up in Christ, uniting in faith, knowledge and maturity, striving to reach the measure of the stature of Christ. The ultimate end is the fullness of Christ dwelling in their hearts and minds. The bride of Christ is made complete by striving, for she has been brought to fullness.

Gifts In Action

I might sound a bit biased, but after visiting hundreds of congregations over the years, I am persuaded we have one the greatest church families in the brotherhood. For more than a decade we have held classes and had seminars on Spiritual Giftedness. We are truly Gift-Oriented in our mindset.

The result is that we are incredibly active in so many ways and productive in leading others to Christ. When one is hurting, we reach out immediately. When one rejoices, we all rejoice together (Romans 12:15). We are on cruise control with our Spiritual Gifts, ready to move into action for whatever arises. I have been offered positions with other congregations, but find it difficult to leave such a productive people in Christ. We are growing in the fullness of Christ as a group and I know God is pleased with the outreach.

8) To Bring Glory to God

1 Peter 4:10-11, *"As each one has received a {special} gift, employ it in serving one another, as good stewards of the manifold grace of God. Whoever speaks, {let him speak,} as it were, the utterances of God; whoever serves, {let him do so} as by the strength which God supplies; so that in all things God may be glorified through Jesus Christ, to whom belongs the glory and dominion forever and ever. Amen."*

Glorifying God is the job description of every Christian. Through these gifts which God has provided, the world *"sees our good works and glorifies our Father in heaven"* (Matthew 5:16). Our entire mission as the saved, sanctified people of God is to bring multiple offerings of glory to God's throne. He gave us these gifts and we have an obligation to use them for His glory.

The Dying Encourager

Ken lived in a small Midwestern town. He suffered from learning disabilities and was dying from brain cancer in the local hospital. For weeks I had studied with him, aiming for conversion, but to no avail. He was a janitor at the area school for more than thirty years, not because he enjoyed cleaning, but because he loved to encourage kids. He was an extreme Encourager.

With time running out, I decided to pull out all the stops. If he enjoyed encouraging children, then I would speak his language. I brought my young daughters to the hospital to encourage him. When Ken saw them, his face lit up with a smile. His heart melted as they interacted. That was the language he spoke fluently!

From there I built upon how much God wanted him as a child of God. Through a few more studies, Ken was ready to be baptized into Christ. Four of us held Ken's wheelchair when we lowered it into the pool at the local hotel. There were some children of the members in attendance at his baptism. I observed an encouraging smile on his face as he made eye contact before going into the water. He later told me that it felt great to be a child of God and that this brought him great joy.

Ken died three weeks later, but with a church family right next to him. As he faded and was unable to control his movements, my daughters rubbed lotion on his hands and put salve on his cracked lips. We sang hymns of encouragement to him (Colossians 3:16) and kept reassuring of the hope awaiting (1 Thessalonians 4:18). His funeral was a joyous occasion of celebration.

In the children's wing of a hospital in Eastern Europe there is a room filled with cribs for orphans. It was named after him and was funded by his memorial fund. It is always about the glory of God when it comes to the Spiritual Gifts. As the Christian hymn states:

Lord, prepare me to be a sanctuary,
Pure and holy, tried and true.
With thanksgiving, I'll be a living sanctuary for You.

Chapter Three

Defining the Spiritual Gifts

There can be much confusion and misrepresentation as to the Spiritual Gifts of which I have already referred. In order to understand what the Spiritual Gifts are, it is best to first discuss what they <u>are not.</u>

There are two primary types of gifts found in the New Testament, those generally given to demonstrate honor (doron: δωρον) and gifts commonly given to receive back honor (charisma: χαρισμσα). The first type of gift says "I respect you" and the second says "I want respect back from you." The first gift is given as a sacrifice and the second is given with grace in mind. Here are some examples.

Doron: δωρον
- Matthew 2:11, *"And they came into the house and saw the Child with Mary His mother; and they fell down and worshiped Him; and opening their treasures they presented to Him gifts (δωρον) of gold and frankincense and myrrh."* The wise men were not expecting something back from toddler Jesus, but simply wanted to honor Him.
- Matthew 8:4, *"And Jesus said to him, "See that you tell no one; but go, show yourself to the priest, and present the offering (δωρον) that Moses commanded, for a testimony to them."* The leper was to honor God for the cleansing he received at the hands of Jesus.

- Hebrews 11:4, *"By faith Abel offered to God a better sacrifice than Cain, through which he obtained the testimony that he was righteous, God testifying about his gifts (δωρον), and through faith, though he is dead, he still speaks."* Abel wanted to show honor and respect toward God by offering the firstlings of the flock.

I mention *"doron"* gifts only to eliminate them from discussion and move to the *charisma* gifts. These are the gifts which were typically given with the intent to be used to further serve God. Here are some of these examples from the scriptures.

Charisma: καρισμα

- Romans 6:23, *"For the wages of sin is death, but the free gift (καρισμα) of God is eternal life in Christ Jesus our Lord."* God gave us the gift of eternal life with the intention of our service to Him. God has never expected us to waste His investment of eternal life to do as we wish, but to live according to His will (see Ephesians 2:8-10).
- 2 Timothy 1:6, *"And for this reason I remind you to kindle afresh the gift (καρισμα) of God which is in you through the laying on of my hands."* God gave Timothy a miraculous gift through the laying on of Paul's hands. Timothy was to use that gift for the furtherance of the gospel.
- 1 Timothy 4:14, *"Do not neglect the spiritual gift (καρισμα) within you, which was bestowed on you through prophetic utterance with the laying on of hands by the presbytery."* The fact that whatever gift Timothy was given could be neglected indicates that there was an expectation from God attached to it.
- 1 Peter 4:10, *"As each one has received a special gift (καρισμα), employ it in serving one another as good stewards of the manifold grace of God."* Notice the special gift was given to be employed, not unemployed.

In order to properly understand, we must define the two types of *charisma* gifts. According to the Interlinear Bible, *charisma* is defined as the following:

Charisma (khar'-is-mah) from 5483; a (divine) gratuity, i.e. deliverance (from danger or passion); (specifically) a (spiritual) endowment, i.e. (subjectively) religious qualification, or (objectively) miraculous faculty.

Charisma has a dual meaning depending on the context of the word. It is either a **passionate endowment and quality** or **a miraculous faculty and power**. There were two types of *charisma* gifts which God gave the members of the first century church, miraculous powers and non-miraculous ministerial passions. Both of these gifts were to bring respect (glory) to God. The focus of the study is not the miraculous gifts, but the non-miraculous.

Paul entered a discussion on these two types of charisma gifts in 1 Corinthians 12:4-6, *"Now there are varieties of gifts, but the same Spirit. And there are varieties of ministries, and the same Lord. There are varieties of effects, but the same God who works all things in all persons."* We know there are two varieties of *charisma* gifts, those concerning ministerial passions and miraculous manifestations. It will be necessary to define the latter in order not to confuse them with the former.

The Miraculous Gifts
1 Corinthians 12:8-11, *"For to one is given the word of wisdom through the Spirit, and to another the word of knowledge according to the same Spirit; to another faith by the same Spirit, and to another gifts of healing by the one Spirit, and to another the effecting of miracles, and to another prophecy, and to another the distinguishing of spirits, to another {various} kinds of tongues, and to another the interpretation of tongues. But one and the same Spirit works all these things, distributing to each one individually just as He wills."*

Here Paul turned his focus to the miraculous side of the list. The following are the nine miraculous gifts according to his teachings.

1) The Word of Wisdom:

This was the ability to reveal the complete plan of salvation in the most benevolent manner possible. Paul's lesson to the Stoics and Epicureans in Acts 17 was a good example of this gift. He had never encountered a culture quite like that, yet possessed the wisdom to present the gospel like a life-long resident.

2) The Word of Knowledge:

This was the ability to understand the message so as to present it to others. The apostles did not have the advantage of going to the "University of Jerusalem" like the Sanhedrin, yet they were well informed and prepared in the scriptures. This was because Jesus downloaded the miraculous gift of knowledge to give them this advantage. Acts 4:13, *"Now as they observed the confidence of Peter and John, and understood that they were uneducated and untrained men, they were marveling, and {began} to recognize them as having been with Jesus."*

3) Faith:

This is not saving faith, but a faith that moves mountains (Matthew 21:21). The early church leaders needed a miraculous boost in their faith to meet the challenges which were ahead. They had the miraculous gift of faith.

- Acts 16:25, *"But about midnight Paul and Silas were praying and singing hymns of praise to God, and the prisoners were listening to them;"*
- Philippians 2:17, *"But even if I am being poured out as a drink offering upon the sacrifice and service of your faith, I rejoice and share my joy with you all."*
- 2 Corinthians 1:9, *"...indeed, we had the sentence of death within ourselves in order that we should not trust in ourselves, but in God who raises the dead..."*

4) Healing:

This was the ability to supernaturally heal the sick. These were not simple healings like aspirins for headaches or chiropractic adjustments. They healed blind people who never saw, cripples who never walked, and deaf people who never heard. There was no denying they had the power of Christ.

- Acts 3:6-7, *"...Peter said...in the name of Jesus Christ the Nazarene-- walk!' And seizing him by the right hand, he raised him up; and immediately his feet and his ankles were strengthened."*
- Acts 5:16, *"Also the people from the cities in the vicinity of Jerusalem were coming together, bringing people who were sick or afflicted with unclean spirits, and they were all being healed."*
- Acts 8:7, *"For in the case of many who had unclean spirits, they were coming out of them shouting with a loud voice; and many who had been paralyzed and lame were healed."*

5) Miracles:

This is in a greater scope than healing the sick, including restoration of limbs, acts of judgment, and resurrections. They completely defied anything in the physical realm and could not be dismissed.

- Acts 13:11, *"...you will be blind and not see the sun for a time." And immediately a mist and a darkness fell upon him, and he went about seeking those who would lead him by the hand.*
- Acts 9:40, *"But Peter sent them all out and knelt down and prayed, and turning to the body, he said, 'Tabitha, arise.' And she opened her eyes, and when she saw Peter, she sat up."*

6) Prophecy:

This was the ability to inform and edify and at the same time, demonstrate God as Revealer of things to come. It was not something general in nature, but specific, like times, places, people and events.

- Acts 11:28, *"And one of them named Agabus stood up and {began} to indicate by the Spirit that there would certainly be a great famine all over the world. And this took place in the {reign} of Claudius."*
- Acts 21:10-12, *"...a certain prophet named Agabus came down from Judea. And coming to us, he took Paul's belt and bound his own feet and hands, and said, 'This is what the Holy Spirit says: In this way the Jews at Jerusalem will bind the man who owns this belt and deliver him into the hands of the Gentiles.'"*

7) Discerning of Spirits:

This was the ability to discern who spoke truth and who did not. Before the New Testament was complete, anyone could show up at a congregation and say what they wanted instead of what was from God. Without the New Testament scriptures to dispute it, the church would be in trouble. Discerning the Spirits allowed them to know if something was correct or not.

- Acts 5:3, *"But Peter said, "Ananias, why has Satan filled your heart to lie to the Holy Spirit, and to keep back {some} of the price of the land?"*
- I John 4:1, *"Beloved, do not believe every spirit, but test the spirits to see whether they are from God; because many false prophets have gone out into the world."*

8) Tongues:

This was the ability to speak fluently in languages one never studied. In Acts 2:4-13 we find the apostles fluently speaking at least sixteen identifiable languages. When the "scholars" attempted to dismiss their new linguistics by claiming they were drunk, it made no sense at all. It was truly a miracle.

- Acts 2:4, *"And they were all filled with the Holy Spirit and began to speak with other tongues, as the Spirit was giving them utterance."*
- 1 Corinthians 14:18-19, *"I thank God, I speak in tongues more than you all; however, in the church I desire to speak five words with my mind, that I may instruct others also, rather than ten thousand words in a tongue."*

9) <u>Interpretation of Tongues:</u>
This was the ability of being able to interpret what was being spoken in a different language. Just because someone could speak a tongue it did not mean those listening could understand what was being spoken. With this gift the problem was eliminated.

- 1 Corinthians 14:7, *"Yet {even} lifeless things, either flute or harp, in producing a sound, if they do not produce a distinction in the tones, how will it be known what is played on the flute or on the harp?"*

<u>The Early Application of the Miraculous Gifts</u>
The Holy Spirit gave the apostles the words to speak for the spreading of the gospel and the miracles were in place to back up the words. As Mark 16:20 states, *"And they went out and preached everywhere, while the Lord worked with them, and confirmed the word by the signs that followed."* The Lord worked with them through the power of the Holy Spirit and the miracles confirmed it. Hebrews 2:4 says, *"God also bearing witness with them, both by signs and wonders and by various miracles and by gifts of the Holy Spirit according to His own will."*

The apostles appear to be the only ones that had all nine of these gifts. They could however lay their hands on other members of the Church and distribute the various miraculous gifts to the others.

- Acts 6:6, *"And these they brought before the apostles; and after praying, they laid their hands on them."*

- Acts 8:17, *"Then they began laying their hands on them, and they were receiving the Holy Spirit."*
- Acts 19:6, *"And when Paul had laid his hands upon them, the Holy Spirit came on them, and they began speaking with tongues and prophesying."*
- Romans 1:11, *"For I long to see you so that I may impart some spiritual gift to you, that you may be established..."*
- 2 Timothy 1:6, *"For this reason I remind you to kindle afresh the gift of God which is in you through the laying on of my hands."*

Acts 8:18 actually states that *"...Simon saw that the Spirit was bestowed through the laying on of the apostles' hands..."* Simon the sorcerer was so wrapped up into the mystical arts that he sought to open a distributorship of the miraculous gifts. Peter rebuked him in Acts 8:21 saying, *"You have no part or portion in this matter..."* There is NO evidence that others, except the apostles, had the ability to pass the gifts onto others.

The apostles wrote letters to these Churches through the influence of the Holy Spirit (2 Peter 1:21); the Churches kept the letters; the apostles and all those whom they laid their hands on eventually died. All the words of the New Testament were already penned by the time the last of that generation died out. The apostolic authority had served its purpose.

The fulfillment of the ceasing of the miraculous gifts of the Holy Spirit was complete as spelled out in 1 Corinthians 13:8-10, *"Love never fails; but if there are gifts of prophecy, they will be done away; if there are tongues, they will cease; if there is knowledge, it will be done away. For we know in part and we prophesy in part; but when the perfect (το τελειον) comes, the partial will be done away."* The written Word was complete; therefore the miracles had served their purpose.

This gospel message spread throughout the kingdom because it was confirmed by the miraculous gifts of the Holy Spirit.

- 2 Corinthians 12:12, *"The signs of a true apostle were performed among you with all perseverance, by signs and*

wonders and miracles."
- 1 Peter 1:12, *"...those who preached the gospel to you by the Holy Spirit sent from heaven—things into which angels long to look."*
- Romans 15:19, *"...in the power of signs and wonders, in the power of the Spirit; so that from Jerusalem and round about as far as Illyricum I have fully preached the gospel of Christ."*
- 1 Thessalonians 1:5, *"...for our gospel did not come to you in word only, but also in power and in the Holy Spirit and with full conviction..."*

The only reason these miraculous gifts are being discussed in this study is so that the readers will NOT CONFUSE them with the non-miraculous ministerial passions. The miraculous gifts of the past are exactly that...of the past. They were there to confirm the words of the New Testament. The non-miraculous gifts (ministerial passions) of the past are for both the present and the future. The first-century church had them both (1 Corinthians 12:4-5, *"Now there are varieties of gifts (καρισμα), but the same Spirit. And there are varieties of ministries, and the same Lord."*) The church of the first century had the miraculous and non-miraculous gifts. The church today has the proven Bible and the non-miraculous gifts.

[Note: If the purpose of the miraculous gifts were to confirm the words of the New Testament, then how can people today reverse the logic? Many in the religious world are teaching that the words of the New Testament confirms their "miracles". Not only does the Bible not teach it, but this introduces circular reasoning which is not a healthy hermeneutic.]

The Non-Miraculous Gifts
     Romans 12:6-8, *"And since we have gifts that differ according to the grace given to us, {let each exercise them accordingly} if prophecy, according to the proportion of his*

faith; if service, in his serving; or he who teaches, in his teaching; or he who exhorts, in his exhortation; he who gives, with liberality; he who leads, with diligence; he who shows mercy, with cheerfulness."

"And Since We Have Gifts..."

How do we know this is not referring to the miraculous gifts of the Holy Spirit? Look at Romans 1:11, *"For I long to see you in order that I may impart some spiritual gift to you, that you may be established..."* Paul was finally coming to Rome and he was bringing miraculous gifts through the laying on of his hands. As established earlier, the miraculous gifts were dispensed to non-apostles through the personal contact of the laying on of hands. Christianity had spread throughout the Roman Empire when Christians were scattered in persecution (Acts 8:4). It appears that no apostle had yet arrived in Rome as of the writing of the letter, for they were yet to receive it. The gifts Paul referred to in 12:6 must be the non-miraculous.

The "we" is Christ's church. We all have non-miraculous gifts whether we want to acknowledge it or not. I have heard some Christians say they feel they do not have a gift, but their feelings do not dismiss the word of God. *"We have gifts* (καρισμα)*"*.

> *"...that differ according to the grace given us {let each exercise them accordingly}..."*

Praise God that we are not all the same! We may all be cleansed by the blood of the Lamb, but we are not identical. We differ in our gifts, or better understood, our passions. That is important to understand when dealing with each other. We are to use our gifts as God designed for us to use them. Many times Christians are not happy in their service to God because they are not focusing on what God wants them to do.

- Romans 12:6-8, *"...if prophecy, according to the proportion of his faith; 7 if service, in his serving; or he*

who teaches, in his teaching; or he who exhorts, in his exhortation; he who gives, with liberality; he who leads, with diligence; he who shows mercy, with cheerfulness."
• Ephesians 4:11, *"And He gave some {as} apostles, and some {as} prophets, and some {as} evangelists, and some {as} pastors and teachers..."*

In the above two passages we find ten non-miraculous gifts. Based on extensive testing of many thousands of individuals, they breakdown in the following ways.

The Non-Miraculous Gifts or Passions and Their General Percentage

Apostle (The Passion of Missions)	6%
Evangelist (The Passion of Proclamation)	9%
Prophet (The Passion of Confrontation)	3%
Teacher (The Passion of Research)	9%
Exhortation (The Passion of Encouragement)	7%
Shepherd (The Passion of Nurturing)	16%
Mercy Giver (The Passion of Counseling)	17%
Servant (The Passion of Helping)	21%
Giver (The Passion of Charity)	2%
Administrator (The Passion of Organization)	10%

There will be one chapter dedicated to each of the ten ministerial passions (gifts) later on, but for now, I will discuss them in generality. The Apostle Peter recorded in 1 Peter 4:10-11, *"As each one has received a special gift, employ it in serving one another as good stewards of the manifold grace of God. Whoever speaks, is to do so as one who is speaking the utterances of God; whoever serves is to do so as one who is serving by the strength which God supplies; so that in all things God may be glorified through Jesus Christ, to whom belongs the glory and dominion forever and ever. Amen."*

There are two types of Spiritual Gifts: those typically exercised through speaking and those exercised through service. There are Spiritual Gifts which tend to be more objective and others which are more subjective. The following chart will provide better understanding concerning the contrast between the various Spiritual Gifts.

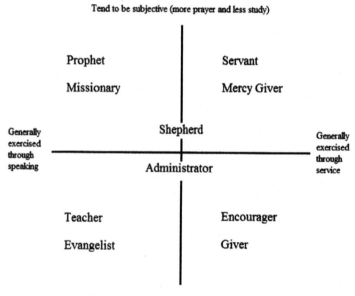

There is a copy of this chart at the back of the book (**see attachment #1**). In the chart you will find the ten Spiritual Gifts in their respective categories. As mentioned by Peter, there are serving gifts and speaking gifts. It is with that we begin the various contrasts of these gifts.

A) <u>The Contrast of Speaking and Serving</u>

The Spiritual Gifts on the left of the chart tend to be exercised through speaking: Prophet, Missionary, Teacher and Evangelist. The Spiritual Gifts on the right side tend to be exercised through serving: Servant, Mercy Giving, Encourager and Giver. The middle two tend to be neutral in that category, being carried out in both speaking and service.

B) The Contrast of Subjectivity and Objectivity

On the top of the chart there are five subjective passions: Prophet, Missionary, Servant, Mercy Giver and Shepherd. People with these passions tend to hold a viewpoint that more reflects their feelings. When a crisis comes into their lives, they have a habit of praying first and studying later. They typically "feel good" before they "fact good."

On the bottom section are the five more objective passions: Teacher, Evangelist, Encourager, Giver and Administrator. They usually hold to a viewpoint which reflects the facts of a situation. When difficulties enter their lives, they tend to study first and then pray. They receive a greater level of comfort when they "fact good" first, leading them to "feel good" about those facts.

C) The Contrast of Mission

There are further contrasts from top to bottom of the chart which reflect the Christian mission of life.

- The Prophet confronts with feelings and the Teacher confronts with the facts.
- The Missionary desires to present the Bride of Christ (Revelation 21:2) and the Evangelist desires to present the Groom Christ (Luke 5:34).
- The Shepherd organizes people and the Administrator organizes plans.
- The Servant ministers with kind deeds and the Encourager ministers with kind thoughts.
- The Mercy Giver shows love through giving their forgiveness and the Giver shows the same through the giving of their funds.

That begs the question, who is right in their approach to Christ? The Prophet, Missionary, Teacher, Evangelist, Shepherd, Administrator, Servant, Mercy Giver, Encourager, or Giver? The answer is…YES. They are all right because each passion is necessary to carry out the mission of Christ.

How to Determine Your Ministerial Passion
Over the years I have determined to take a five-fold approach when assisting someone in determining their Spiritual Gifts. The five steps are as follows.

1) Through a Written Test **(see attachment A)**
The quickest route in identifying a Spiritual Gift would be in the written test. There is nothing scientific about the test except that it categorizes your subjectively provided information into the ten objective gift groups. The entire test should only take about twenty minutes and can provide great insight. You can take the Spiritual Gifts Test online at www.findmyspiritualgift.com.

2) Through The Testimony Of Self **(see attachment D)**
Next to God, you know yourself better than anyone else. As we examine each of these individual passions in detail, rate yourself from 1 to 10 in each of the categories and record the data in attachment #D.

3) Through The Testimony Of Those Who Know Us **(see attachment E)**
The people close to us often see things that we might be blind to. When they know what the gifts are, they may be able to identify which passion fits the best. As you study the ten categories, give the sheet to your spouse, relative, or friend. Have them rate you with the same methods from the self-analysis test.

4) Through The Life Of Christ
If written in detail, the world itself could not contain the books of the wonderful things of Christ (John 21:25). All Christians were attracted to Jesus for certain qualities demonstrated in His life. If one can identify what they love most about Jesus, then it very likely is their gift.

5) Through Years Of Trying Many Different Ministries
Most Christians who have reached an appreciable level of

maturity have done so through sampling the many ministries. They tend to know what generates the most joy, having learned their gift through the experiences of the faithful Christian walk.

The written test is very accurate, but the more ways that a person uses to identify their gifts, the better off and more accurate their assessment will be. Jesus wants our *"joy to be full"* and doing this in the prescribed way will facilitate this goal.

The Secret Shepherd
    In the past we have used this strategy many times with our high school youth groups In one particular instance, we handed out the written test in advance to all twenty-five youth members and then collected the data. We covered each of the individual gifts one week at a time while administering the other four confirmations.
    This brings up Carrie, one of our seniors at the time and the only one of the youth who tested highest in Shepherd. I discussed with the class the detailed description of the qualities of the Shepherd and told them that one person tested highest in it. Upon asking the students to point to the person it best described, simultaneously they all pointed to Carrie.
    I asked Carrie if that described her and she confirmed it did, saying what she loved most about Jesus was the time spent with his disciples. When asked what she liked to do in the church, she provided an example of her organizing the youth to send out the care packages for the soldiers serving overseas. All the evidence indicated she was a Shepherd. At that time I revealed her test results as #1 Shepherd. She scored highest in that category on the written test and received four confirmations in less than fifteen minutes, providing confidence what her passion was.

In Closing:
    There are Spiritual Gifts of ministerial passions. We had them before we became Christians and simply sanctify it to

serve God after conversion. When we know what these passions are, then we will have the joy in our Christian service that God desires in our relationship to Him.

Chapter Four

The Gift of Missions

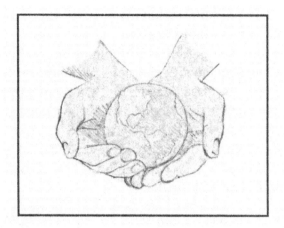

A Basic Understanding Prior To Studying the Gifts
There should be a few understandings before beginning a detailed analysis of Spiritual Gifts. They are as follows:

A) It is possible to have passion in all the gifts, but all the gifts are not equal in passion.
The Christian's life is to be filled with joy. To limit it to one area of Christian service would be foolish. On the other hand, we must understand that only one gift can personally stand out above the others. It may not seem apparent at first, but hopefully it will be by the end of the study.

B) It is possible to have developed talent associated with a gift, but talent is not passion.
There are many things that we are good at that really do not produce joy. It is a true statement concerning employment, "A person should do what he really enjoys instead of simply working for a paycheck." There have been many great people with great talents, but that did not mean they were passionate about it. The same goes for Christians in their service to Jesus, for one can be talented in one area of giftedness without experiencing real joy.

C) It is possible to have joy with one, but still have responsibility in all of the gifts.

A person can go through life doing only what they most enjoy and neglect other Christian responsibilities. Just because someone has the passion to Serve does not mean they can neglect the need of Encouragement for a saddened saint. Just because someone may passionately enjoy Teaching, this does not relieve him or her of the responsibility of Giving and Serving. Though we seek to have joy, we strive to become complete in areas of weakness.

With these three points in mind, let us begin the study of each of the ten gifts and discover which one is our greatest passion. They will be covered in detail, including the signs of maturity, immaturities and practical application.

1) Apostle -The Passion of Missions (Ephesians 4:11)
Ephesians 4:11 "And He gave some {as} apostles..."

Only about 6% of people have this passion. What is an apostle? It is the Greek word apostolos (αποστολοσ) meaning "one that is sent out, a messenger." An apostle of Jesus was one who was an ambassador of the gospel of Jesus Christ.

The word most generally refers to "the apostles." Jesus chose twelve men to be His handpicked messengers or apostles. Mark 3:14 reads, *"And He appointed twelve, so that they would be with Him and that He could send them out to preach..."* Jesus said in John 6:70, *"Did I Myself not choose you, the twelve, and yet one of you is a devil?"* It was to Judas whom Jesus referred. He betrayed our Lord and was removed from the twelve. Later, after Judas killed himself, he was replaced with another, as we read in Acts 1:26, *"And they drew lots for them, and the lot fell to Matthias; and he was added to the eleven apostles."*

From that moment they were "the" (definite article) twelve

apostles. They all shared the unique characteristics of having been with Jesus from the *"beginning with the baptism of John until the day that He was taken up"* in the ascension (Acts 1:21-22). The only exception to "the apostle" rule was Paul. He was personally added by Jesus as an *"apostle born out of due time"* (1 Corinthians 15:8-9).

It is unquestionable that the primary reference to "apostles" in the New Testament is to "the apostles" of Jesus. The definite article phrase "the apostles," refers to the apostleship 39 times in the New Testament (for example Acts 1:25; Rom. 1:5; 1 Cor. 9:2; Gal. 2:8). It must have been the common meaning among the first-century church members. Some examples of this is the following:

- Acts 1:2, *"...until the day when He was taken up, after He had by the Holy Spirit given orders to the apostles whom He had chosen."*
- Acts 2:37, *"Now when they heard {this} they were pierced to the heart, and said to Peter and the rest of the apostles, 'Brethren, what shall we do?'"*
- Acts 4:33, *"And with great power the apostles were giving witness to the resurrection of the Lord Jesus, and abundant grace was upon them all."*
- Acts 15:6, *"And the apostles and the elders came together to look into this matter."*
- Jude 1:17, *"But you, beloved, ought to remember the words that were spoken beforehand by the apostles of our Lord Jesus Christ..."*

Though the word generally refers to a specific group called "the apostles," one would do well not to associate every use of the word in the same way. There is also the missionary use of the word in the New Testament. Here are some of those examples.

- In Acts 14:14 both Paul and Barnabas are called "apostles," but Barnabas was not listed among "the apostles."

- Romans 16:7 refers to Andronicus and Junias as "apostles" even though they were not among "the apostles."
- In 2 Corinthians 8:23, Titus and two unnamed brothers that were "sent out" to spread the gospel were called αποστολοσ, translated "messengers."
- In Galatians 1:19, James the brother of Jesus is called an "apostle," even though he did not believe in Him until after the resurrection (John 7:5).
- Philippians 2:25 lists Epaphroditus the αποστολοσ, translated "messenger," but does not list him among "the apostles."
- 1 Thessalonians 2:6 refers to Paul, Timothy, and Silas as "apostles," even though the latter two were not among "the apostles."
- Hebrews 3:1 refers to Jesus as "the Apostle." This was because He was "sent out" by God (John 17:3, 20:21).

The context of the listed examples refers to one being "sent out with a message" and not "the apostles." Therefore, the context of the word refers to "missionaries" and not "apostleship."

The same appears to have occurred in Ephesians 4:11 in referring to the "gifts" given to members of the church for the equipping of the saints. To read it and jump to the conclusion that the word αποστολοσ from this verse refers to "the apostles" or "apostleship" would not be reasonable. If we translate instead of transliterating the word "apostolos," the verse reads this way: *"And He gave some {as} sent out messengers, and some {as} prophets, and some {as} evangelists, and some {as} pastors and teachers..."*

God is not the *author of confusion* (1 Corinthians 14:33) and would have likely lined up appropriate miraculous gifts with the ministerial passions. If this is true, then the missionary would have likely possessed the gifts of tongues and the interpretation of tongues, for it would have aided them well as they traveled to all of the different regions of the Empire. When the miraculous gifts were phased out with the canonization of the New Testament, only the passion would have remained (see chapter 3). Today we use a more modern word for those with the passion of the *"sent out messengers"*; they are called *missionaries*.

Who is the Missionary?

He is one who deeply desires to start congregations where none exist. His or her passion is to facilitate the formation of churches despite the world of ignorance or hostility to the Lord. The Missions passion beckons one to *"Go therefore and make disciples of all the nations..."* (Matthew 28:19-20). This passion drove the first century church to spread *"...both in Jerusalem, and in all Judea and Samaria, and even to the remotest part of the earth"* (Acts 1:8).

The Missionary possesses the unique ability to consistently hold a worldview of Christ and the church. His sense of adventure does not stop at the neighbors, for he must *"Go into all the world and preach the gospel to all creation"* (Mark 16:15). The person with the well-developed gift of Missions is not afraid to march into Satan's backyard and begin sharing the Word of God for the further expansion of the church.

They are passionately persuaded this is their calling in life. Missionaries want to turn *"...the world upside down..."* (Acts 17:6) through the spreading of God's word. John 4:35 says, *"Do you not say, "There are yet four months, and {then} comes the harvest'? Behold, I say to you, lift up your eyes, and look on the fields, that they are white for harvest."* With reaping tools in hand, one with the gift of Missions deeply desires to go to these fields and reap the harvest.

Signs of Maturity
    A)   <u>They Are Visionary.</u>
        1)   They are not intimidated by obstacles.
        2)   They generally hold a worldview of Christ and the Bible.
        3)   They are risk takers.

When working among a culture different from our own, it is important to hold to the Word without being distracted by the world. We all are told in 1 John 2:15a, *"Do not love the world nor the things in the world."* The individual with the mature Missionary passion is able to hold to the worldview of Christ while incorporating the culture into Christ. They understand that the gospel of Jesus was designed to seamlessly drop in to any culture of any time.

The Missionary with a Vision

Gerald Paden was an instructor at one of the preaching schools I attended. He was also the one in charge of testing the potential mission teams for Spiritual Giftedness. Before our survey mission trip to Romania, Gerald took us through his course and allowed us to see our potential. I asked him what his Spiritual Giftedness was and he told me Teacher / Missionary. I had no idea how mature his passion was until finally learning more about his past.

During the Cold War he was a fulltime missionary in Italy, leading many to Christ, including dozens of priests. He was so successful in converting souls in this prominently Catholic environment that the Italian Supreme Court kicked him and his brother out of the country for a year. When the government finally agreed to allow him back in, he continued the work exactly where he left off, but not without resistance.

When Gerald finished his stint in Italy, he took a teaching position with Sunset International Bible Institute (SIBI). His duties were not limited to teaching students attending the school in Lubbock; he was also permitted to teach on many of the SIBI campuses throughout the world.

While working in Iowa in the late nineties, I met a brother from the Hickman Road Church of Christ named Francesco. He was a convert from Italy through the work of Gerald. Brother Francesco shared with me the story of his conversion through the efforts of Brother Paden, as well as many other stories of Gerald's passion for the work in Italy. The excitement in the voice of Francesco was contagious. At that moment it was fully confirmed to me that Gerald had a mature passion of a Missionary decades before I met him.

B) <u>They Are Adaptable.</u>
  1) Culture
  2) Language
  3) Foods
  4) Travel

These traits are extremely important when dealing with cultures different than our own. I am actually very low in this passion, but high in Evangelist and Teacher. I participate in overseas missions to preach and teach, for that is what drives me. After a month I am always anxious to come home, being unable to adjust to the culture and missing the comforts of our culture. The one with the passion of Missions adapts much more easily to the new culture, allowing them to continue for the long run.

Paul captures this trait in 1 Corinthians 9:20-23, *"To the Jews I became as a Jew, so that I might win Jews; to those who are under the Law, as under the Law though not being myself under the Law, so that I might win those who are under the Law; to those who are without law, as without law, though not being without the law of God but under the law of Christ, so that I might win those who are without law. To the weak I became weak, that I might win the weak; I have become all things to all men, so that I may by all means save some. I do all things for the sake of the gospel, so that I may become a fellow partaker of it."* He was willing to adjust to whatever circumstance and for various types of people.

The Flaming Missionary

There is a sister in Christ in our home congregation who tested extremely high in this category, but we already knew this. She was always trying to have us go out after worship for various ethnic foods. One morning following worship, she asked if we wanted to go out to lunch for African food…two hours away!

She was continually up for the challenge in Missions, even learning sign language and taking the lead in our Deaf ministry. She accompanied us on one foreign mission trip and likely will make more in the future. Over the years, I have seen her grow into a much more mature servant with her passion of Missions because she embraces what truly gives her joy.

    C) They Are Non-Materialistic.
        1) They generally have modest possessions.
        2) They are not interested in material gain.
        3) They know the Lord will make the ends meet.

Being non-materialistic is a trait that serves one well with the Spiritual Gift of Mission. A change in culture typically means a sacrifice of worldly comforts. For the person who is led into foreign fields, it possibly means losing items like electricity, running water, and the Internet. Because travel for both foreign and domestic work is common, it is actually made much easier to prepare and make these trips with limited possessions, supplies and comforts. They are used to having little because it weighs them down in their goals and also can generate a spirit of jealousy among the populace with which they live.

Trust In the Lord
For many years my wife and I supported a missionary family in India. The head of the family was named Prassad. He was a graduate of the Kakinada School of Preaching and had a deep passion for Missions in his own country. His choice of ministry was in Hyderabad, India. He was reaching out to the orphans and other local downtrodden children of the community. It was hard work, but it paid off as he was able influence many. He could have made more money preaching for a larger congregation in a more comfortable area, but he decided to do

the more difficult task.

He had a wife and three children whom I had the pleasure of meeting on one trip to the region. His choice of mission had caused the living standard for his family to slip. His children had rather worn clothing nurtured by the love of a good mother. Reaching out to the poor kids in the neighborhood meant sacrifice for his own family, but he was content, knowing that God would provide for them in the end.

Moved by such a passionate spirit of Missions, I told them, "God will provide today!" I was able to raise some extra funds for the trip to spend for Prassad's family. I took all five to the market to purchase new clothes and shoes for them. Seeing his children in new garments and his wife with a new sari, he smiled and looked up to heaven, saying, "Thank you God for this blessing!" He trusted in the Lord like the mature Missionary he was. He did a great work because he embraced his true passion of the Missionary.

Signs of Immaturity

Peter remarks in 1 Peter 2:1-3, *"Therefore, putting aside all malice and all deceit and hypocrisy and envy and all slander, like newborn babies, long for the pure milk of the word, so that by it you may grow in respect to salvation, if you have tasted the kindness of the Lord."* When someone becomes a Christian, they tend to bring some of their baggage with them into Christ. Through many years and experiences, Jesus helps them unpack their flaws and put the baggage away. Until that time a person tends to exhibit more immature qualities. Here are some of these signs of immaturity which more easily identifies a person with the Spiritual Gift of Missions.

A)   They Are Impulsive.
        1) They are often unorganized.
        2) They are often underfunded.
        3) They are often untrained.

I have noticed that people with the passion of Missions often tend to be low on Administration. I do not know why, but it is a pattern. When this occurs, disaster often follows. Planning out a new mission is much more complex than just buying a plane ticket and having a passionate love for Jesus. One must network, raise funds, strategize a curriculum, provide for costs, and make connections. Jesus said in Luke 14:28, *"For which one of you, when he wants to build a tower, does not first sit down and calculate the cost to see if he has enough to complete it?"* The immature individual with the passion of Missions often will not weigh up the true costs, leading him down a turbulent path.

The Unprepared Missionary

Years ago there was a man in a local congregation who wanted to become a missionary in a foreign country. He was always active in the church and loved it when the overseas missionaries visited. On one of those visits, he decided to begin the transition into the mission field. Without any formal training, without the funds raised, and without having ever gone on a survey trip, he sold his possessions, put in his resignation to his employer and began to the process of moving to Haiti. Needless to say he never made it there, for he had the immature passion of a Missionary without the planning of an Administrator.

   B) They Are Impractical.
       1) They tend to set goals too high.
       2) They tend to move too fast.
       3) They tend to do too much.

The immature one with the passion of Missions tends to be impractical. Their passion to hit the mission field is so great in the beginning that they fail to allow reality to catch up. When this occurs, they tend to double down, thinking it to be a lack of effort. If they are not careful it might cause them to give up.

The Overzealous Newbie

More than a decade ago, a young couple moved into our congregation. They were recent graduates of one of the brotherhood universities and the husband was extremely passionate about Missions.

Three months later, the young man called a meeting with our elders and myself. In the conference, the young man said that he would like to start an inner-city congregation on the other side of the river. He was requesting to take about ten families, rent a property, and begin evangelizing the area. He was extremely sincere, but sincerely wrong in the method. A church plant requires much more planning than simply grabbing some families and holding a worship service. I reminded him that the main priorities of the church is to bring lost souls to Christ and to keep them faithful. With one simple question the reality set in for the young man. I asked, "Brother, how many people have you led to Christ in your twenty-three years on this earth?" He lowered his head and replied, "None." Commending him for his passion, I explained the need to mature in the areas which will best serve his passion, then plan big. I involved him in some of the ministries and he was nurtured along.

A few years passed and they moved to the Pacific Northwest with the intent to make a difference for the kingdom. The problem was that he had yet to lead one soul to Jesus, making him completely inexperienced to do that which he felt a calling to do. He gathered some other couples he knew from college and set up a home church. Three years passed, no one was converted and even a couple of families fell into unfaithfulness. The movement disbanded in failure, not because of a lack of passion, but from a lack of maturity.

C) They Are Impatient.
    1) They can be impatient with old converts.
    2) They can be impatient with new converts.
    3) They can be impatient with non-converts.

I have been on many mission trips in the past and have witnessed the impatience of the immature Missionary numerous times. When demonstrating their inexperience, the impatience becomes obvious. Their high octane can burnout the converts who are already part of the congregation, cause new converts to feel they cannot keep up, and keep others from wanting to accept the challenge to convert.

<u>The Impatient Missionary</u>
While writing this chapter and sipping a decaf coffee in Starbucks, I met two men sitting across from me. Being a flaming Evangelist, I could not resist starting a conversation with them. Their names were Greg and Bill.

Greg was a very religious, former Vietnam veteran, having an extreme passion of Missions. He had been to Brazil on a trip about two decades ago and decided to attend missionary training from an area school. Our conversation revealed that he really had no set destination, no set time of departure, and no set plan for evangelizing. He felt a calling for Missions, but was completely unprepared.

His friend Bill remained rather quiet until Greg departed for home. At that point he truly opened up to me. He said, "I am nothing like Greg, he has kind of gone off the deep end with this spiritual adventure." He further explained that he liked Greg, but could not understand how he could be so disorganized in his approach to life. It is sad when even his best friend could not substantiate Greg's immature approach to his ministerial passion of Missions.

Some ways to obtain joy with this gift
A) Take a foreign mission trip.
    This will most definitely allow you to see to what level you are a Missionary.

B) Start a Deaf ministry in your own congregation.
    Because this reaches out to people different than you, it might likely satisfy the need.

C) Raise support among the congregation for outside mission work.
There are many responsibilities in missions. Perhaps you cannot go to the mission field, but you could help send someone to go in your place.

D) Be active in the organization and participation of local missions.
These are all missions which can be done without relocation. They include food banks, clothing closets, and other ministries.

E) Pray for specific mission teams across the globe.
Solicit the prayers of the fellow saints concerning the world-wide mission work.

F) Email, write, and send surprise gift packages to foreign mission teams.
This can be done with short notice, low cost, and high effectivity. It also can pull others into the ministry. Years ago there was a group of Mission-minded ladies who made quilts and sent them with me for the dying orphans in Eastern Europe. The excitement they shared in doing so was contagious for the whole community.

G) Conduct door-knocking campaigns, home Bible studies, and inner-city work.
The key factor here is that you are reaching out to people different than yourself. That is what drives the Missionary. One does not have to go overseas to reach out to people different than us. There are Indian reservations, Spanish populations, Appalachian poverty and Deaf communities, all of which are missions.

Finally!
During my first mission trip to Africa, one of the financial supporters from our congregation was named Dru. She is an

extremely patient and loving sister who has a deep passion for Missions. For many decades she has spent her summer vacation to volunteer at Manatawny Bible Camp, ministering to the young children and sharing in the adventure. She was overjoyed when I told her of my mission to a western region elementary school in Ghana. She had always wanted to do something like that, but had been in a decade-long battle with cancer.

Still, I wanted to nurture her passion of Missions, so I brought her back a nice Ghanaian souvenir to put on her shelf to keep that passionate fire warm in her heart.

A few years back she came out of remission to fight another battle with cancer. I encouraged her to win that battle, and Lord willing, she would go on the next mission trip. She did beat it after countless prayers and chemo.

At the time of the writing of this chapter, I am preparing for another mission to Greece. While there, we will be involved with a ministry teaching English to Afghan women and children who are refugees from the war. Dru, now dealing with her third bout of cancer, is going to be making that trip with my wife and me. We are convinced that her strong desire to go be involved in foreign missions is one of the reasons that she is still here. It brings tears to my eyes in anticipation of the smile on her face as she patiently teaches a young Afghan orphan how to speak and write in English.

Her passion for a culture different than hers will always be an example for me and others long after she passes. She might not be long for the world, but her Spiritual Gift of Missions will be sweetly satisfied in the days to come.

Chapter Five

The Gift of Evangelism

Evangelist – The Passion of Proclamation (Ephesians 4:11)

Ephesians 4:11 *"...And He gave...some {as} evangelists..."*

Only 9% of a congregation has the passion of Evangelism. How is Evangelist defined? The word is *"euangelistēs"* (εὐαγγελιστής) and it means to be "a bringer of good tidings." What specifically is the "Good News?" It is the gospel of Jesus Christ.

What is the gospel of Jesus Christ? As Paul so eloquently explained in 1 Corinthians 15:1-4, *"Now I make known to you, brethren, the gospel which I preached to you, which also you received, in which also you stand, by which also you are saved, if you hold fast the word which I preached to you, unless you believed in vain. For I delivered to you as of first importance what I also received, that Christ died for our sins according to the Scriptures, and that He was buried, and that He was raised on the third day according to the Scriptures..."*

This gospel message of the death, burial, and resurrection of Jesus Christ was the awesome first-century message that some of the populace received, took a stand on, were saved by, and held fast to. Romans 10:15 asserts, *"And how shall they preach unless they are sent? Just as it is written, 'How beautiful are the feet of those who bring glad tidings of good things!'"* *(KJV)* It is the good news that Jesus was confirmed the *"Son of God with power"* (Romans 1:4) through the *"resurrection from the dead."* We do not have to live in the guilt and doubt of sin, but have eternal life. Jesus, the Son of God, the Lamb of God, with the Spirit of God, came and offered Himself on the cross for God as the substitute for our sins (1 John 2:2). We do not have to die in our sins (John 8:24), but have eternal life (John 3:16). We don't deserve it; we can't earn it; we must accept it as a gift if we are to have it.

It is good news because we can take God up on this offer, *"not by works lest any man should boast"* (Ephesians 2:8-9), but through the passive, submissive surrender of a believing baptism (Mark 16:16; Acts 2:38). It is through the *"washing of regeneration and renewing of the Holy Spirit"* that God's mercy touches and changes us (Titus 3:5). We make an appeal to God for a good conscience through this resurrection because He has laid it out for the taking (1 Peter 3:21). When you look at it from that perspective, THAT IS GOOD NEWS! AMEN!

Like a newspaper boy calling out the headlines from the street, the evangelist deeply desires to put forth the message of the resurrected Jesus. "EXTRA! EXTRA! READ ALL ABOUT IT! JESUS' TOMB FOUND EMPTY! HOPE PREVAILS!" As Paul summarized this passion in 1 Corinthians 2:2, *"For I determined to know nothing among you, except Jesus Christ, and Him crucified."* The passion of the Evangelist communicates *"...for woe is me if I do not preach the gospel"* (1 Corinthians 9:16). The one with the true passion of the Evangelist MUST share that message with others.

Many Share the Passion of the Evangelist.

There are many in the Bible who demonstrated a passion of Evangelism. Here are just a few:

- God Himself had the passion. Galatians 3:8, *"And the Scripture, foreseeing that God would justify the Gentiles by faith, preached the gospel beforehand to Abraham, {saying} 'All the nations shall be blessed in you.'"* (KJV)
- Jesus had the passion. Luke 20:1, *"And it came about on one of the days while He was teaching the people in the temple and preaching the gospel, that the chief priests and the* scribes with the elders confronted Him..." (KJV)
- Paul had the passion. Romans 1:15, *"Thus, for my part, I am eager to preach the gospel to you also who are in Rome."* (KJV)
- Timothy had the passion. 2 Timothy 4:5, *"But you, be sober in all things, endure hardship, do the work of an evangelist, fulfill your ministry."*
- Many of the disciples of the first century church had this passion. Acts 8:4, *"Therefore, those who had been scattered went about preaching the word."*

Signs of Maturity
   A) They are personable.
       1) They generally get along with others.
       2) They generally are more tolerant of others.
       3) They generally are more upfront with others.

The one with the passion of the Evangelist has often been compared to the salesmen and women of the body of Christ. Nobody is a stranger to the person with this Spiritual Gift. I speak of this not from theory, but from experience, because this is my number one passion in Christ. We do not like to take "No" for an answer; we will be persistent when it comes to proving the *"evidence that the Christ had to suffer and rise again from the dead"* (Acts 17:3). They will take on the challenge when prompted!

<u>The Front Step Surprise</u>

As mentioned, I LOVE evangelism! That introduces us to Brad Johnson, a good friend of mine, and a flaming Servant. He was extremely low in the passion of Evangelism, but willing to do some door-knocking in an area trailer court to invite others to a Bible study. He wanted me to make the first few calls to see how it worked. I knocked on five of them and spoke with four people. From that we have successfully invited three people for a study.

I must emphasize that door-knocking for one with the passion of Evangelism is like Christmas morning to the young child. Behind every door is a prospect for conversion. The Evangelist is not afraid of who might come to the door, knowing that the next person might become a new brother or sister in Christ. Starting a conversation comes very easy for me.

Brad saw how easy it really was and decided that he was ready for a try. He walked up to the door of one of the homes and knocked. He had a smile on his face as he heard the footsteps of the alerted owner inside. The door popped open and a man bearing the resemblance to Charles Manson's love-child stepped out. He took one look at Brad and yelled, "My lot rent is overdo; my girlfriend left me; I lost my job and I'm out of cigarettes! What do you want?"

Brad was speechless. Nearly soiling himself, he turned his head and looked at me, then back to the man and then back to me. He wanted nothing to do with the predicament. I stepped up to the broken man, extending my hand to greet him and said, "What you are saying is that you are having a horrible day, right?" The man had the look of a deer in the headlights. He stared at me, smiled and then laughed, saying, "You got that right!" I responded, "That is why we are here. We bear good news."

Over the next forty-five minutes we sat on his deck and visited with him concerning his life. I shared some Bible verses and he agreed to another study. Upon leaving I gave him a "man hug" and let him know that Jesus can change so much for him. It brought him comfort.

After our departure Brad made it clear that door-knocking was not for him. What brought great excitement to me was a big stress for him. We might have both been saved by the blood of Christ, but clearly his passion for Evangelism was not the same as mine.

    B) <u>They are motivating.</u>
        1) They are expressive in speech.
        2) They are extravert in personality.
        3) They are extreme in persuasion.
        4) They are energized in work.
        5) They are expectant in goals.

<u>A Truly Motivational Speaker</u>

When I think of the passion of Evangelism, many people come to mind. One in particular was a motivational speaker named Richard Rogers. He was a longtime instructor at Sunset International Bible Institute and a former mentor of mine. I met him for the first time while attending the Tulsa Soul Winning Workshop in the 1990s. Richard was speaking to a group of about three-thousand on the topic of being evangelistic in our core being.

Having not grown up in the church and not having been exposed to any large scale events such as this, I was in "Evangelism Heaven." There were many lessons on evangelism from some of the top names in the brotherhood over the course of several days. My energy level was on an all-time high, but it would be the lesson Richard preached which caused me to make a lifechanging decision.

He came to a point in his lesson which dealt with the passion he had for the gospel of Jesus Christ. During the climax of the sermon, he quoted 1 Corinthians 9:16, *"For if I preach the gospel, I have nothing to boast of, for I am under compulsion; for woe is me if I do not preach the gospel.* " Brother Richard spoke about the impossibility of stopping him from preaching the death, burial, and resurrection of Jesus. It went like this...

> "If the government came and threatened me to stop preaching Jesus, I would do it anyway. If they cut out my tongue, then I would be Deaf signing the gospel with my hands. If they cut off my hands, then I would tap dance in Morse code with my feet. If they cut off my feet, then I would write the gospel in the dirt with my nose, *for woe is me if I do not preach the gospel of Christ!*"

I said to myself, "This brother gets it!" After the lesson I went up to Richard and introduced myself, thanking him for the inspiring lesson on the gospel. I told him that was exactly how I felt about Jesus' death, burial, and resurrection. After visiting a little more, he encouraged me to come to SIBI and become a full-time worker for Christ.

Two years later, sitting in a classroom at Lubbock, Texas, I was studying at the feet of Richard and many other great men of Christ. It was there that I received my initial formal training for preaching and it was one of the greatest decisions of my life. This would not have come about had it not been for a man with the burning passion of an Evangelist.

C) They are vocal.
1) They love to talk about the crucifixion.
2) They love to talk about salvation.
3) They love to talk about eternity.

Breaking the Silence

Back in 2001 on one of my mission trips to Romania, I ended up teaching a bit too long and literally lost my voice. This had never happened and I was rather concerned. Ray Kesler, the head of the work in Ploiesti, decided to take the day off and make a trip by train to Bucharest. My plan was to rehydrate and keep my mouth quiet for a twenty-four hour period. (It was killing me!!!) Ray was doing all the talking and I was basically participating in the day through mute observation.

As the day drew to a close, it was time to take the train back to Ploiesti. We booked a nice seated room in the train car, being shared with one younger woman headed to Brasov. Ray and I are rather large men and we do not look like Romanians, so naturally the lady inquired what we were doing in the country. Ray said we were there for mission work in Ploiesti, helping the people and sharing the gospel of Christ. He was doing a good job for someone with the passion of Administration, but I was itching to say something more about Christ.

The young lady explained that she was a second year law student and on her way to visit some family. I simply listened quietly for the sake of my vocal cords, but was yearning to talk about the gospel. Then, as if God was placing a golf ball on the tee awaiting a whack with a club, the lady asked the most tempting question I have ever heard. She questioned, "What is so good about the gospel?"

Beyond the grace of God I don't know how it happened, but somewhere deep down inside the excitement swelled in my heart and pressure filled my lungs! I began to make my attempt to speak. At first it was just air whisking through my larynx, and I was only mouthing the words. Bearing down a little more, I engaged the vocal cords, sounding a bit like Freddy Krueger with a Bible. Within about fifteen seconds, my throat cleared and I was in a full-blown death, burial, and resurrection lesson of a four-alarm gospel presentation! Ray was rather surprised to hear me not only speak, but express passion in the words!

I was on cruise control, sharing the message of hope. By the time we reached our destination, the lady was very encouraged, being able to see the value of the message. She still needed to continue another hour to her stop, but Ray told her of a congregation to look up in Brasov. She agreed to do so and hopefully followed up. What became of her we did not know, for I was going to be heading home after a few days. One thing for sure, the seeds of the gospel were deeply planted and would hopefully be ready for watering (1 Corinthians 3:6).

Signs of Immaturity
    A) They are emotional.
        1) They tend to be up and down.
        2) They tend to be overly expressive.
        3) They tend to be loners.

The immature passion of the Evangelist can often be overtaken by his emotions. Their drive to communicate the gospel of Jesus is so passionate that they forget others might not feel the same way about it as the others around them. When that reality finally catches up, they might become entangled with these emotions, feeling rejected. They also expel so much energy in their presentation that they need to get away from others. I experienced this for many years following a long day of preaching and teaching. One way to combat the fatigue was to take a drive out in the country and be away from everyone just to put my thoughts back in my head.

    B) They are impulsive.
        1) They tend to be impatient.
        2) They tend to interrupt conversations.
        3) They tend to act without thinking.

To the immature Evangelist, there is a need to force people to see the cross instead of allowing them to do so. They might view questions as challenges to the message and cut people off a bit too early. Some people take many months and even years to respond to the gospel, but the babe in Christ with the passion of Evangelism tends to rush it.

Baptism! Baptism! Baptism!

There is a story about a young preacher who had a deep passion for the gospel. Every sermon he preached was about the death, burial, and resurrection and baptism into Christ. This went on for about six months and some of the members of the congregation grew frustrated. The elders had a meeting with him and emphasized the need to also cover something else from the Bible besides the gospel. The preacher said, "Okay," and promised to teach a different sermon the next week.

The following Sunday morning he announced the title of his sermon, "*Lessons from Noah and the Ark.*" He went into detail of the prevailing wickedness of mankind and the need for God to wipe them out. He explained further about the construction of the ark, the falling rain, and the rising water. Pausing for a moment, he revved up his voice, "Now that we are talking about water, let me tell you what Peter said about baptism and that ark in 1 Peter 3:21!"

You get the point. Telling an immature Evangelist to talk about something other than responding to the gospel is like telling a baby not to cry. It can often take years to mature past that point with the gift of Evangelism.

    C) <u>They are intense.</u>
        1) They tend to push others too hard.
        2) They tend to be insensitive.
        3) They tend to overwork.

Bully for Christ

I was baptized into Christ in June of 1988 after more than a year of searching for the truth in the Bible. From day one I was extremely zealous to share the gospel with as many people as I could. The first couple of years after my conversion, I drove more people from Christ than I led to Him because my immaturity.

Evangelists are debaters, but if one is not careful, he can become a debater who poorly represents the cause of Christ (Colossians 1:20). When I would be sharing the gospel with people and they just refused to see the simple message of salvation, the level of debate would elevate. I would become somewhat of a gospel bully, cutting down what they believed instead of persuading them to see why I believed what I did. Thank God I learned from my immaturities and pressed on to better practices.

Some Ways to Obtain Joy with This Gift

A) Door-knocking Campaigns
   Evangelists typically love this because of the enjoy meeting new prospects and are quick in starting conversations.

B) Home Bible Studies With the Lost
   The Evangelist is at home in the home of others, for that is his office. Crossing the threshold of the door opens the heart to the gospel.

C) Short or Long-term Foreign Mission Trips
   Many areas in the world are more receptive to the gospel of Jesus. Many conversions can keep the evangelistic batteries charged for the Evangelist.

D) Studies With Young Christians
   Immediate follow-up with the recent converts will keep them faithful.

E) Preaching Sermons
   Their fire for the death, burial, and resurrection might be the thing which ignites the passion of evangelism for the whole congregation.

F) Teaching Classes That Are Christ-Centered
   Everything the Evangelist teaches goes back to the cross of Christ.

Back Door Evangelism

Cline Paden was a famous missionary, the director of a preaching school, and a flaming Evangelist. His work was legendary for leading many thousands to Jesus Christ in his lifetime. It is a particular story from his door-knocking days which peaked my interest the most. He was in a neighborhood knocking doors for Bible studies when he came upon a very irate man. The man yelled at Cline, attempting to intimidate him and oppress the gospel message of Jesus. It ended with the man slamming the door in Cline's face.

Brother Paden did not let it get him down. He simply went to the back door of the home and knocked. When the man came to the door, he looked at Cline in disgust and said, "What do you want?" Cline calmly responded, "I came to the back door because the man at the front door was so mean. I was hoping the guy in the back was much kinder." Not only did that quick and bold decision pave the way for a Bible study, but also the man's conversion. That is truly the passion of Evangelism in action!

Chapter Six

The Gift of Confrontation

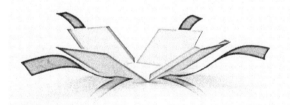

Prophet –The Passion of Confrontation (Romans 12:6; Ephesians 4:11)

Romans 12:6, *"And since we have gifts that differ according to the grace given to us, {let each exercise them accordingly} if prophecy, according to the proportion of his faith;"*

Ephesians 4:11, *"And He gave some... {as} prophets..."*

Only about 3% of a congregation tests highest in this gift. The word *prophet* in the Greek is *pro*, meaning "fore or front" and *phemi,* meaning "to make known one's thoughts." Vines Expository defines this word as "one who speaks forth or openly." Without controversy, the primary definition of the word is in reference to the miraculous foretelling or exposing information to take place based on revelation from God.

The first-century church had the miraculous gift of prophecy, as well as eight other miraculous gifts. They were in lieu of the New Testament which had yet to be completed. When John the apostle died, being the last survivor of the twelve, the transfer of the gifts would not have continued. They were bestowed through the "*laying on of the apostles' hands...*" (Acts 8:18).

The Roman Christians apparently were not established in this area, for Paul remarked in Romans 1:11, "*For I long to see you in order that I may impart some spiritual gift to you, that you may be established...*" They were in the same position concerning the miraculous gifts as the disciples in the region of Ephesus (Acts 19:1-6). Verse 6 said, "*And when Paul had laid his hands upon them, the Holy Spirit came on them, and they began speaking with tongues and prophesying.*"

The miraculous side of the gifts, however, would have died out with the completion of the New Testament. 1 Corinthians 13:9-10, "*For we know in part, and we prophesy in part; but when the perfect comes, the partial will be done away.*" Just because the miraculous gifts of wisdom, knowledge, and healing were done away with, did not mean that the fervent desires of Evangelism, Teaching, and Mercy died out with it. The ministerial passions were possibly linked in this way to the miraculous gifts. "*Now there are varieties of gifts, but the same Spirit. And there are varieties of ministries, and the same Lord*" (1 Corinthians 12:4-5).

The Prophet on a Donkey

A couple of thousand years ago in Israel, an old man was riding on a donkey. He rode past a young man up in a tree, sawing a branch. The problem was the tree trimmer was actually sitting on the limb which he was cutting. The old man on the donkey yelled up to the young man, "Sir, you should not sit on the branch which you are sawing, for you could have a bad fall." The young man was prideful and harshly responded, "Don't tell me how to trim a tree. My father was a tree trimmer and his father before him. My three uncles, two cousins, and brother were also tree trimmers. My best friend is a tree trimmer. Keep your advice to yourself!" He had forgotten that *pride comes before a fall* (Proverbs 16:18).

The elderly man on the donkey replied, "Okay, have a nice day" and rode away while the young man continued sawing. A couple of minutes later, the old man on the donkey heard a loud crash. He looked back to find the chap lying flat on his back next to the severed branch. The dazed man came to his senses, stood up, and pointed to the old man on the donkey, saying, "Stop that man, for he is a great prophet!"

The Passion of the Warning

Of course you get the point. The passion of the Prophet, or the one with the gift of confrontation, is very similar to the prophets of old, minus the miraculous manifestation. In the same way that Ezekiel and John could not digest the scroll and the little book in Ezekiel 3 and Revelation 10, the individual with the passion of confrontation cannot digest the knowledge of the sin in the culture around them. They internalize and try to process the ills of the world, but it must come back out of their mouths to confront those around them.

Their message is not from miraculous revelation, but through continual meditation on God's word. Their passion leads them to *"have their senses trained to discern good and evil."* (Hebrews 5:14) They are the filters and sensors of the congregation concerning sin and spiritual danger. They are, in every essence, the fire alarms of the church, warning of impending danger ahead.

Have you heard of the phrase "non-confrontational"? This does <u>not</u> describe the prophet, for they are definitely confrontational. It isn't that they want to confront, but that they <u>must</u> confront. They deeply desire for the Word of God to be known and will not sit around to allow others to perish without knowing what is at stake.

When Peter shunned the Gentiles, Paul had no problem confronting him: *"But when Cephas came to Antioch, I opposed him to his face, because he stood condemned"* (Galatians 2:11). Paul demonstrates the passion of Confrontation with action!

The Prophet knows that someone has to step up and confront. He or she takes the unique message of what will happen if the course of sin does not change. They have the ability to keep the importance of repentance at the forefront of their mind. In this way, they share a trait with the miraculous prophets of old, for "they know the future" consequences for those who do not heed the word of God. The following verses are typically great motivation for the prophet.

- Revelation 2:5, "Remember therefore from where you have fallen, and repent and do the deeds you did at first; or else I am coming to you, and will remove your lampstand out of its place-- unless you repent."(KJV)
- 1 Peter 3:12, "For the eyes of the Lord are upon the righteous, and His ears attend to their prayer, but the face of the Lord is against those who do evil."
- James 5:19-20, "My brethren, if any among you strays from the truth, and one turns him back, let him know that he who turns a sinner from the error of his way will save his soul from death, and will cover a multitude of sins."
- 2 Peter 2:21, "For it would be better for them not to have known the way of righteousness, than having known it, to turn away from the holy commandment delivered to them." (KJV)
- Amos 4:12, "…prepare to meet your God, O Israel."

Signs of Maturity
    1)   They are *Discerning.*
        A) They are sensitive to sin.
        B) They are "black and white" thinkers.
        C) They are steadfast in their position.

Typically, seeing everything in "black and white" is one of the biggest signals that one has the passion of confrontation. The Prophet finds great comfort in the rules and will not budge very easily from his positions. They tend to sit on the right side of the congregation, about two-thirds up, have their arms folded, and scrutinize every word you say. They do this not because they don't care, but because they <u>do</u> care very much about what is being taught in the assembly.

Snortin' Wharton

One of my favorite people on earth is a man named Ed Wharton. He has been a teacher of preachers for more than a half-century, having trained several thousand with his sound teaching. He was one of my instructors in school back in the '90s and remains one of my mentors to this day. He earned the nickname "Snortin' Wharton" because of his firm approach to backing up what is taught in the scriptures. He is an extreme Teacher/Prophet.

This was never so apparent to me than in one of my preaching labs. He could be brutal. I wanted to be ready for his critique, so I began making preparations early on. My assignment was to preach on the Book of Titus. I decided to memorize the entire book word for word just to be able to defend my points. I was determined to earn an "A" from this brother.

The day finally arrived for me to preach my sermon. Ed pulled out his pen and laid an evaluation sheet on the table. I started my lesson and everything was going smoothly. About two-thirds of the way through the sermon, I proof-texted a point. All of a sudden a puzzled look came over Brother Wharton's face, indicating that he was questioning the validity of my point. He rapidly grabbed his Bible and began thumbing through it with a determined pace, checking to see if what I was said was true. Holding his finger on a verse on the page, I could see him nodding in approval. It was so obvious that he was in "Prophet Mode." I paused and said, "Did you confirm it was true, you flaming Prophet?" He just laughed, and I continued on to the end of the sermon. And yes, I received the "A" in the end.

    2)   They are <u>*Decisive.*</u>
        A)   They are candid in conversation.
        B)   They are convicting in confrontation.
        C)   They are consistent in correction.

    Nobody is as candid as the Prophet among the Spiritual Gifts. Sometimes they can be brutally honest when they confront, but it is still done out of love. Mature Prophets are not fickle when it comes to sin, for it can never be sugar-coated.

<u>The Power of the Prophet</u>
    Back in the '90s I met a gem of a sister named Mildred, who happened to be a member of our local congregation. Within approximately 30 minutes after meeting and conversing with her, I could tell, without a doubt, that she was a Prophet. She was deeply concerned about the decline of our culture and how it can creep into the church. She truly grieved over the sin of the world and clearly understood that eternal death was the result (Romans 6:23). Later on, when our congregation was covering Spiritual Giftedness, my observation was proven correct. She took the written test and scored off the chart in the Prophet category.
    When dealing with someone as passionate as Mildred, it is always important to take great heed to their words, even if you do not agree with their point. This was never clearer to me than one Sunday morning after my sermon when Mildred gently pulled me aside. In a soft voice, she asked, "So Doug, do you think it is okay to cuss in your sermon?"
    Immediately my heart sunk, thinking I might have let a word slip among the other five thousand preached from the lesson. I responded, "My goodness, did I say a cuss word? What did I say?" She looked left and then right, as if to make sure nobody was listening to what she was about to repeat. She softly

whispered, "You said *golly*." My natural thought was, "Are you kidding, you extreme Prophet? You think '*golly*' is a cuss word?" My actual response was the Prophet-friendly, "What do you mean?"

Mildred explained, "Doug, when we use cuss substitutes, are we not desensitizing ourselves and the church family to the real cuss words?" I did not agree with her, but said, "Let me think about this Sister, and I will attempt to reconcile it in my head. Perhaps you are onto something." She thanked me, and I headed home for lunch.

I was absolutely not in agreement with her point, thinking it was too legalistic. Then, on the drive home, I started thinking about what she said. Would I want my children using cuss substitutes like "Darn it" and "Shoot?" Of course not, as it would be irresponsible parenting. Then I thought of the verse, *"Let no unwholesome word proceed from your mouth, but only such a word as is good for edification according to the need of the moment, so that it will give grace to those who hear"* (Ephesians 4:29). By the time I reached home, I realized that she was right.

I informed my family at the dinner table of the need to be careful about "cuss substitutes," because it could lead to other undesirable speech. Though Mildred is long gone, I think of her whenever writing a lesson or preaching a sermon, knowing that her ministerial drive taught me that all words really have meaning. She was a mature Prophet who taught me well.

3)   They are *Disciplined.*
    A)   They tend to live righteously.
    B)   They tend to pray continuously.
    C)   They tend to study regularly.

The mature Prophet tends to live a disciplined life because they are sensitive to sin. They pray often and study regularly, which tends to train their consciences to properly discern. Of all the maturities among the gifts, the Prophet strives to live by the rules.

The Weeping Prophet

One of the most fervent prophets I know would be Sister Leola. Though she is a loving and caring Christian, her conviction of confrontation tended to lead some into the perception that she was disgruntled. Prophets are often viewed by others in this way.

When we had the Spiritual Giftedness class, she tested highest in Prophet. Wanting to further confirm the results, I asked her if she wept over the sins of others. Leola went on to say that she prayed every morning in the shower, often weeping until the hot water was gone. She did this so others in the home did not know of the tears she shed. She said the sorrow was so great that her husband actually had to put in a larger hot water heater to accommodate the need. I was intrigued to know this and felt that her passion could be of great use to the church family.

Often times prophets experience turmoil in their lives when they are misunderstood. The pressure in the presence of sin can be so great that, by the time they speak up, it comes across as abrasive. Leola was no exception. We strategized how to be more sensitive to others in her confrontations, and she agreed to work on it. We agreed that if she would filter her words prior to saying anything, then she could be more effective.

It did not take long until one of these opportunities arrived. One of the sisters from our congregation disappeared off the radar, having missed many weeks in a row because of some issues she was going through. I asked Leola if she could pray about it and then stop by to bring that sister back. Sure enough, the next week she returned.

I spoke with Leola after the worship service. She said that after praying and weeping for the erring sister for a couple of days, she finally worked up the courage to drive out for a visit. She drove around the block about a half dozen times, working up the courage to go up to the door. Finally, she pulled up in front of the house and knocked on the door. When the sister answered, she was greeted by a tearful Leola, hearing the words, "I miss you and want you to come back to the fellowship." The erring sister's heart melted, and they embraced one another. She demonstrated her repentance and came back to the church family. Leola ended up being a great tool in the hand of the Lord for the congregation there because she finally understood and embraced her ministerial gift.

Signs of Immaturity
1)   They have Rough Relationships.
     A)   They tend to be judgmental.
     B)   They tend to be dominant.
     C)   They tend to be insensitive.

When there is immaturity in the life of the Prophet, WATCH OUT! They are the most judgmental people you can encounter. This is typically demonstrated in display of a negative attitude about all the ills of the world. They will crush you with their hardcore positions and not take into consideration other people's opinions.

Prophet in Denial
During the first night of a weekend seminar back in 2005, I covered the Prophet category for the last lesson. Staying around to visit for about forty-five minutes after the conclusion, I noticed there was a silent, yet anxious-looking woman waiting to speak to me. She was a small, middle-aged sister who finally worked up the courage to talk with me.

Her name was LuAnn, and she had a few questions concerning the testing. She exclaimed, "I have a complaint concerning the written test, for it says that I am a Prophet. I simply refuse to believe this." Examining the results, I could see that she tested nearly maximum in that category and the next closest score was half that amount. I asked her why she felt it was not accurate. She said the description of the Prophet did not sound flattering to her. She did not like to be labeled in that way.

I decided to take the time to re-ask the eight questions from the test pertaining to the Prophet and she answered them the same way as before. I told her that it was correct, having taken her subjective feelings and putting the input into objective categories. She very adamantly proclaimed, "I simply do not agree with you; I do not have the gift of confrontation!" I could see this conversation risked getting out of control and the pressure was mounting.

I calmly responded with a smile, "Sister, you waited forty-five minutes to confront a gospel preacher twice your size to argue against data you provided, and you tell me that you are not a Prophet? That has flaming Prophet written all over it." She quickly retorted, "But I don't want to be a Prophet!"

LuAnn went on to explain that she had often felt like an outsider in the congregation because other members viewed her as a legalist and sometimes a complainer. I encouraged her with the truth by reminding her that the person with the passion of confrontation is a valuable asset to the congregation. I explained that a Prophet will speak up when a warning is needed, while many others in the group might remain silent.

Over the next half-hour, we discussed some of the many jobs for her within the present ministry goals of the local congregation. The one that she was most drawn to was starting a ministry to reach out to troubled teenage girls of the community, knowing they needed firm guidance. By the end of the conversation, she was more than happy to accept who she was in Christ.

A few months later, I received a nice gift package in the mail. After opening it, I discovered it was a handwritten note from LuAnn. It read: "Greetings from your favorite Prophet. I wanted to thank you for pointing me in the right way. I am using my gift to serve the Lord in my congregation. I am filled with hope and joy. Thank you so much and enjoy your gift of appreciation." I also had great joy knowing that she was making the transition from immaturity to maturity in her passion from God.

2) <u>They are Intimidating Teachers.</u>
   A) They tend to be opinionated.
   B) They tend to be prideful.
   C) They tend to be over-demanding.

We all must beware of confronting an immature Prophet, for they tend to defend their opinions to the death. This leads to pride, and pride leads to a fall. What can make it even worse is when they begin to impose their viewpoints on others without discussion. I have found the best thing to do in cases like that is to smile and say, "I love you because you are such a flaming Prophet!" This disarms them and opens the door for growth.

<u>The Recovering Confronter</u>
During the first year of my minister position in Pennsylvania, I received a call from a former member of our congregation who wanted to meet with me for a visit. Getting together at a restaurant, he told me he left the congregation about five years prior because they were "going liberal." I asked him, "What happened after that?" He told me a story of jumping from one congregation to another and from town to town, resulting in having to worship in his home with his wife and children. This is a major sign of an immature prophet who refused to grow up in Christ. They are often isolated as a result of their bad behavior.

Another sign of immaturity for those with the gift of Confrontation is what I refer to as "litmus testing." They begin firing questions like, "What do you think about this issue?" They seek to find the areas of disagreement with the goal of expressing their opinion with pride. This brother was no exception, and I was not going to empower him in his immaturity.

Shifting into "Prophet-defensive" mode, I listened carefully, spoke slowly, and tried very hard to agree when possible. On about the fifth question, I inquired of him, "Did you know you are an immature Prophet?" He did not know what I meant and DEMANDED an explanation!

I expounded that his ministerial passion was the gift of Confrontation and that he needed to be careful to use it wisely for God. I emphasized the need to choose battles wisely or risk being a stumbling block to all he comes into contact with. The discussion ended with me showing him the great value he could be to a congregation, but only if he allowed his gift to mature. He agreed to examine the course, take the test, and strive to do better in the future. And yes, he tested out as a Prophet.

A few years later while doing the seminar at another congregation in our state, I ran into the brother. He had been attending the fellowship for more than a year and was doing better in his personal relationships. No longer was he as aggressive in his approach to others, but was *swift to hear, slow to speak and slow to wrath* (James 1:19). It has been many years since then, and he is still at the same congregation and interacting better with them. Yes, he is still a Prophet, being willing to warn of danger on the horizon, but his confrontations do not stand in conflict with others like they used to.

3)   They have Erratic Emotions.
     A)   They tend to be depressed.
     B)   They tend to be angry.
     C)   They tend to be pessimistic.

There is nothing sadder than watching a Prophet's gift wither away through depression. The "my way or the highway" approach often leads them down that path. Their anger grows and is then transferred to others. The immature Prophet is the most pessimistic person by far. When attending the Spiritual Gifts seminar, they tend to not even want to take the test because it is a new concept for them. [Note: They forget that there are four other tests that can be administered without them even knowing. If you run into this in your congregation, make sure to use these methods to identify them.]

Ten Spiritual gifts: The Gift of Confrontation

Born a Prophet, Die a Prophet

I knew a widower named Martin, who was one of the most negative brothers I have ever encountered. He was an outright pessimist. Though he had been a Christian for decades, he was still an immature *babe in Christ* (1 Corinthians 3:1). After nearly every sermon I preached, there was Martin, negatively remarking about it and picking me apart.

Since two-thirds of the Bible is Old Testament, I tend to preach two-thirds of the time from that section of Scripture. While doing a series on the Sacrificial System from Exodus and Leviticus, Martin complained that he was a New Testament Christian and did not need the Old Testament. I asked him, "Do you remember Lot's wife?" He replied, "Why?" I reminded him that Jesus <u>commanded</u> in Luke 17:32 to *"Remember Lot's wife."* How can we do it if we fail to read the Old Testament? He simply would not listen.

During a visit at his place, I gave him the Spiritual Giftedness test. It confirmed to me that he was a Prophet, but he manifested the gift into a curse. This type of angry spirit of immaturity did not allow many people into Martin's life. He suffered from depression and loneliness because if it.

His own family would not visit him because of his judgmental attitude. Those in the church were very cautious to approach him. He would often not be in contact with anyone for days when going on one of his tirades. It was during one of these times that he went missing for about a week. When his family went to his house, they discovered that Martin had been dead for more than five days. His lack of wanting to mature in this area of his life was very apparent. I had a horrible feeling in my heart while preaching his funeral. It was not because I believed he wouldn't be in heaven, but because he had squandered his gift for God.

Some Ways to Obtain Joy with This Gift:

   A)   Practice a confrontation ministry.

        This ministry works by allowing you to be the one that goes after the wayward souls of the congregation. It is best to team up with a Mercy Giver or Encourager to have a balanced approach. One confronts and the other comforts.

B) Start a prayer ministry for the lost.
    Others need to be motivated through your serious prayers over the danger that awaits the erring soul.

C) Celebrate and congratulate repenting sinners who are coming back to the Lord.
    It is always important to be there to show approval when a sinner repents. Your hugs and encouragement will be warmly received.

D) Spend much time with new Christians.
    New Christians need guidance to stay away from danger. Take them under your wing and teach them to be sensitive to sin.

E) Teach a class on the importance of Christian living.
    Nobody can teach this type of lesson with more passion than the Prophet.

F) Become involved in a prison ministry.
    Often prisoners are living in denial of their bad actions. They fail to make the connection to the natural consequences of their negative behavior. The Prophet will be frank and honest with them, hopefully helping them to accept responsibility.

Chapter Seven

The Gift of
Teaching

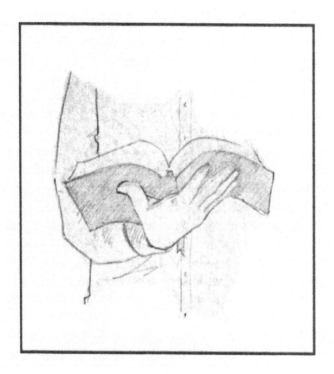

Teacher—The Passion of Teaching (Romans 12:7; Ephesians 4:11)

Romans 12:7, *"...he who teaches, in his teaching..."*

Ephesians 4:11, *"...and some {as}...teachers"*

About 9% of a typical congregation has the passion of the Teacher. The word for teacher in the Greek means "one who instructs." The Teacher is the one who is able to transfer to others what he or she has learned from research and experience. The true gift of Teaching is different than just assuming the responsibility of instructing a class. There are many who teach but do not test high in this Spiritual Gift. Talent does not mean giftedness, but giftedness can always lead to talent.

The Inner Drive of the Teacher

As the gold miner diligently searches to find treasure from the ground, the gift of Teaching compels the individual to sift through the mounds of information in search of gems of valuable knowledge. They desire to *"search the scriptures daily"* (Acts 17:11 KJV) in search of truth. Like a hungry infant, they *"...long for the pure milk of the word..."* (1 Peter 2:2). It is as David spoke in Psalm 119:103, *"How sweet are Your words to my taste! Yes, sweeter than honey to my mouth!"* Teachers long to pass their treasure on to others so that they might share the joy of discovery. This act of sharing brings a Teacher his or her greatest pleasure concerning the kingdom of God.

As mentioned in previous chapters, the words of the New Testament were confirmed by the miraculous gifts (Mark 16:20). Those with the passion of a Teacher were likely endowed, through the laying on of the apostles' hands (Acts 8:18), with the miraculous gift of knowledge. When the words of the New Testament were penned in their entirety and the last apostle had passed on, the presence of miraculous gifts here on earth came to an end. 1 Corinthians 13:8 states this specifically concerning the miraculous gift of knowledge, *"...if there is knowledge, it will be done away."* That leaves only the ministerial passion of Teaching to remain. There were many in the Bible who demonstrated this drive, and by examining a few examples, we can better understand this gift.

Jesus was called "Teacher" more than anyone else in the New Testament. Whenever you read in the New Testament that Jesus was called "Master" or "Teacher," it is the same word used by Paul. Jesus is referenced 42 times as Teacher. This is because *nobody* taught like Jesus.

- The people recognized Jesus as a teacher. In Matthew 7:28-29, the result was that *"when Jesus had finished these words, the multitudes were amazed at His teaching; for He was teaching them as {one} having authority, and not as their scribes."*

- The Scribes called Jesus "Teacher". Matthew 8:19, *"And a certain scribe came, and said to Him, 'Teacher, I will follow You wherever You go.'"*
- The Pharisees called Jesus "Teacher". Matthew 9:11, *"And when the Pharisees saw {this,} they said to His disciples, 'Why is your Teacher eating with the tax-gatherers and sinners?'"*
- The rulers called Jesus "Teacher". Matthew 19:16, *"And behold, one came to Him and said, 'Teacher, what good thing shall I do that I may obtain eternal life?'"*
- The Herodians called Jesus "Teacher". Matthew 22:16, *"And they sent their disciples to Him, along with the Herodians, saying, 'Teacher, we know that You are truthful and teach the way of God in truth, and defer to no one; for You are not partial to any.'"*
- The Apostles called Jesus "Teacher". Mark 4:38, *"And He Himself was in the stern, asleep on the cushion; and they awoke Him and said to Him, 'Teacher, do You not care that we are perishing?'"*

It appears that everyone who met Jesus recognized Him as being the passionate Teacher. Would it not make sense that His own church should also recognize the same? If we identify Jesus as "Teacher," does that not then make us His students? If we are, indeed, His students, does that then also mean we have the obligation to listen and apply His words to our lives? Of course it does!

In imitation of Christ, Paul also demonstrated the passion of the Teacher. Here are further examples.

- 1 Timothy 2:7, *"And for this I was appointed a preacher and an apostle (I am telling the truth, I am not lying) as a teacher of the Gentiles in faith and truth."*
- 2 Timothy 1:11, *"... for which I was appointed a preacher and an apostle and a teacher."*

- Philippians 3:5-6, *"... circumcised the eighth day, of the nation of Israel, of the tribe of Benjamin, a Hebrew of Hebrews; as to the Law, a Pharisee; as to zeal, a persecutor of the church; as to the righteousness which is in the Law, found blameless."* [Note: Being a Pharisee meant that Paul was deeply committed to the scripture, having the first five books of the Law memorized.]
- Acts 22:3, *"I am a Jew, born in Tarsus of Cilicia, but brought up in this city, educated under Gamaliel, strictly according to the law of our fathers, being zealous for God, just as you all are today."* [Note: Only the up-and-coming scribes could study under the top teachers.]
- 2 Peter 3:16, *"... as also in all his (Paul's) letters, speaking in them of these things, in which are some things hard to understand, which the untaught and unstable distort, as they do also the rest of the Scriptures, to their own destruction."*

We Are Also to Be Teachers Whether or Not That is Our Primary Gift.

Even if something is not our primary passion, we still have the responsibility to help out in areas in which we might not be passionate. The same applies to teaching.

- Titus 2:3-5, *"Older women likewise are to be reverent in their behavior, not malicious gossips, nor enslaved to much wine, teaching what is good, so that they may encourage the young women to love their husbands, to love their children, to be sensible, pure, workers at home, kind, being subject to their own husbands, so that the word of God may not be dishonored."*
- 1 Timothy 4:11, *"Prescribe and teach these things."*
- 1 Timothy 6:2, *"And let those who have believers as their masters not be disrespectful to them because they are brethren, but let them serve them all the more,*

because those who partake of the benefit are believers and beloved. Teach and preach these principles."

- 2 Timothy 2:2, *"And the things which you have heard from me in the presence of many witnesses, these entrust to faithful men, who will be able to teach others also."*
- Hebrews 5:12, *"For though by this time you ought to be teachers, you have need again for someone to teach you the elementary principles of the oracles of God, and you have come to need milk and not solid food."*

<u>We Are to Teach With Care.</u>

With our responsibility, we have the great requirement to do our best for Jesus and the church. Therefore, we must teach with great care and diligence.

- James 3:1-2, *"Let not many {of you} become teachers, my brethren, knowing that as such we shall incur a stricter judgment. For we all stumble in many {ways.} If anyone does not stumble in what he says, he is a perfect man, able to bridle the whole body as well."*
- 1 Timothy 1:3 (KJV), *"As I besought thee to abide still at Ephesus, when I went into Macedonia, that thou mightest charge some that they teach no other doctrine..."*
- 2 Timothy 4:3 (KJV), *"For the time will come when they will not endure sound doctrine; but {wanting} to have their ears tickled, they will accumulate for themselves teachers in accordance to their own desires."*

Signs of Maturity

When individuals with this Spiritual Gift reach maturation, they become a great asset to the congregation. They possess the ability to ground the church in the Scriptures. A mature Teacher is able to *"hold fast the faithful word which is in accordance with the teaching, so that he will be able both to exhort in sound doctrine and to refute those who contradict"* (Titus 1:9). Here are some of the traits of a developed passion of Teaching:

1) <u>Their Study</u>
   A)   They are diligent in research.
   B)   They are deep in knowledge.
   C)   They are dynamic in presentation.

Their passion compels them to research the Bible. Week after week and year after year, they accumulate a deep knowledge of the Holy Scriptures and the application thereof. They teach with a deep conviction that motivates others to change minds and actions.

<u>The Administrator/Teacher</u>

Before he had to move as a result of a job change, Brian was an elder at Camp Hill. Though Administration is his highest gift, Teacher is a close second. It was this powerful combination of passions that made him one of the best leaders our congregation has ever had. His lessons were superb, his research diligent, and his knowledge deep. I am convinced that he could easily give up his secular career and work full-time in ministry.

When our leadership wanted to develop a curriculum for going through the Bible in less than a year, it was Brian who spearheaded a new project to do so. He spent many hours each week preparing a top-notch curriculum, and delegating to a responsible team of proof-readers, teachers, artists, marketers, and other needed personnel. He even recorded an audio edition for those who wanted to download the material and listen to it in their car. The new curriculum was a great success and is now being used by other congregations in the brotherhood. Though a team effort, in reality it was the passion of an Administrator/Teacher put into action.

2)   Their Stability
    A)   They are firm in their position.
    B)   They are factual in their feelings.
    C)   They are faithful to the Bible.

The one with the passion of Teaching "facts good," then "feels good." They are not prone to subjectivity and existential feelings, knowing the Word of God is complete. They believe *the sum of God's word is truth* (Psalm 119:160) and will only change their position when it is warranted by the Bible.

Little Girl, Big Passion

Passions are present before conversion, and they are sanctified after entering into covenant with Jesus. This was never as evident as it has been in my oldest daughter, Natalie. When she was in kindergarten and learning to read, she would come home and pretend to be a teacher to her three-year-old brother. With her little chalkboard, she would spell out the words learned from the day's lesson at school. Her little brother thought he was in class and actually learned to read before preschool.

Throughout her childhood, Natalie often said she wanted to be a school teacher. By the time she was seventeen, she was already a trainer for Denny's restaurants. She was training many men and women more than twice her age. Upon graduation from high school, she not only went on to become a school teacher, but actually won the Teacher's Scholarship from the local school district. And yes, today she teaches young children in the same youth group she grew up in. She has striven to mature in her Spiritual Gift of Teaching.

3)   Their Satisfaction
    A)   They are content with context.
    B)   They are comfortable with the truth.
    C)   They are calmed with the Word.

The mature Teacher finds great comfort in opening up a Bible and accepting what it says. They do not feel compelled to manipulate the Scriptures but are satisfied with *"...handling accurately the word of truth"* (2 Timothy 2:15).

Brother Ted

I had the pleasure of studying under Brother Ted Stewart at SIBI. He was EXTREMELY passionate in Teaching. His lessons were detailed, his knowledge was great, and his dedication to the Word was focused. He would consume any book in front of him, attempting to understand the deeper things of God. It was only natural that he also owned a local book store, the natural environment of the Teacher.

When I first met him during a class, he demonstrated his passion by lugging in several books. He always seemed to have a small library in his arms while walking the halls of the school. Brother Ted was determined to know the answers to tough questions and would often spend many hours in research to find a truth. Sometimes I would catch him at his desk with a book open, a finger on the text, and a serious look on his face.

One afternoon during our class, he did not show up. All the students waited for him to come, but after fifteen minutes we started studying other material. When the dean of the school came into the room, he asked, "Where is Ted?" We explained he did not arrive. The dean called Brother Stewart at his home. The conversation went something like this...

Dean: "Hey Ted, what are you doing today?"
Ted: "I am calculating the number of years from the Shepherd Kings to the Exodus."
Dean: "Did you have somewhere else you needed to be right now?"
Ted: "Let me think..."
Dean: "What do you teach on Tuesdays?"
Ted: "Oh, that's right! I have a class right now! I will be right over."

Brother Ted was so engrossed in his studies that he forgot our Bible class that day. He still showed up with his many books, apologizing as he came in. With the remaining fifteen minutes he taught a great class and I was still pleased. The years have passed and although he has gone on to be with the Lord, his writings and teachings are still relevant to the brotherhood, the school, and my life. He had a mature gift of Teaching and he used it for God.

Signs of Immaturity
1)   Their Complexity
    A)   They tend to use too much detail.
    B)   They tend to do too much studying.
    C)   They tend to expect too much.

When one is mature in the passion of Teaching, he or she can be an incredible asset to the church. When the person refuses to develop their passion, the consequences can become disastrous as the following example illustrates.

Overkill!
Many years ago, a congregation I was familiar with hired a new preacher who was working on his PhD. Since the church was located in a university town, they felt he would be a good fit to reach out to the "educated elite" of the community. Nothing could be further from the truth, for he was a flaming Teacher, but extremely low on Evangelist.

One of the early warnings of his immaturity was his dissertation on the Book of Ephesians. When he sent it to the school for a first submission, they sent it back, informing him to eliminate another 500 pages! Ephesians is only a six chapter book! Obviously, he was in overkill mode.

About a month into his ministry, he announced his desire to do a Sunday evening series on the Book of Ruth. He spent six months covering a four chapter book. The attendance for Sunday evenings dwindled. He was teaching at a university level to people who could not digest it. His lessons were not practical for the members of the congregation and, as a result, they grew very weary.

His lack of evangelistic drive resulted in no converts. He was not a bad guy and his intentions were not evil, but his days in preaching were numbered. He grew frustrated that the church family did not embrace his overly-deep knowledge of the Word. When he announced that he would be starting a series on the Book of Job, a forty-two chapter book, his fate was sealed. In less than a year, they fired him and the congregation suffered from a split from which it took them years to recover.

What would have happened had the preacher hiring committee employed the knowledge of the Spiritual Gifts course in their recruiting efforts? How might it have turned out had the congregation used Spiritual Giftedness to encourage the brother in the right way? What if the young preacher used Spiritual Giftedness to adjust his teaching in order to effectively meet the needs of the congregation? I am convinced it would have turned out better for everyone.

2)   Their Conceit
  A) They tend to be prideful.
  B) They tend to be critical.
  C) They tend to be intolerant.

When the passion of Teaching fails to develop, conceit will surely follow. History is littered with former followers of Christ who fell victim to their folly. They forgot the words of Paul from 1 Corinthians 8:2-3, *"If anyone supposes that he knows anything, he has not yet known as he ought to know; but if anyone loves God, he is known by Him."* The immature teacher has a great potential to destroy the souls of many, including his own (James 3:1).

The Prideful Teacher

Jim was a relatively new Christian and took great pride in his interpretive skills of the Scripture. He spent countless hours memorizing texts, analyzing the Greek, and learning the deep truths of the Bible. He grew in all the areas valuable for a teacher, except in the application of his knowledge. He was very critical of others when they taught. As 1 Corinthians 8:1 states, *"knowledge makes arrogant."* Jim came across as nitpicking and intolerant to any opinion which might be different than his. After nearly every sermon, he cornered the preacher in the lobby, saying, "I have a disagreement with you!" He also had a tendency to engage in arguments about issues that did not amount to anything.

As a result of this behavior, Jim was not well received by his fellow saints. The elders were very reluctant to allow him to teach a class until he was more mature. In the end, Jim was offended and decided the elders were obviously "unscriptural" in their position. He left the congregation for another. After repeating this cycle three more times, he is no longer a faithful Christian and refuses to meet with others of the faith. 1 Corinthians 13:11 states, *"When I was a child, I used to speak like a child, think like a child, reason like a child; when I became a man, I did away with childish things."* Jim refused to grow up in Christ with his passion of Teaching and ended up putting his own soul in danger.

3) Their Conscience
   A) They tend to be aggressive.
   B) They tend to be anxious.
   C) They tend to be angry.

The Teacher with immaturity can be very aggressive towards his or her church family. Even worse, they often use the Word of God to seemingly back up their incorrect arguments. When this happens, it not only makes the family of God look terrible, but also portrays the Word of God as inconsistent.

Confessions of a Flaming Teacher

This is my second highest Spiritual Gift, falling only slightly behind Evangelist. When I was a new Christian, I poured over the scriptures for many hours each day, wanting to know as much as possible. As a result, I gained a lot of knowledge about the Bible, but still had great immaturity in knowing how to apply this knowledge.

In Bible discussions, I was very aggressive, wanting to prove what I believed as true. Whenever I heard someone *"teaching things they should not teach"* (Titus 1:11), it greatly upset me. I deemed it my personal responsibility to defend the truth. I came across as aggressive in my efforts to stomp out false teaching, *"earnestly contending for the faith which was delivered unto the saints"* (Jude 3). I constantly relied on one tool from my toolbox – a sledgehammer. It took a long time until I was able to deal with people in a more loving and gentle way.

1 Timothy 1:5 states, *"But the goal of our instruction is love from a pure heart and a good conscience and a sincere faith."* I could lovingly confront with the truth instead of bullying my way into an argument. Over the years I have worked rather hard at maturing my passion of Teaching. My goal went from winning arguments to winning souls, and I have never looked back.

Some Ways To Have Joy In This Gift

A)   Engage in a steady regimen of exegetical study (the tearing apart of verses).
     This will challenge the individual to new levels in their study. Exegetical study allows the Word to *"...richly dwell within you, with all wisdom"* (Colossians 3:16).

B)   Commit to memorization of the Scriptures.
     Memory work allows the potency of the Word to permeate all thinking and behavior. This will also assist

when teaching others, being able to quote the passages with confidence.

C) Read one Biblically centered book every couple of weeks (commentaries, studies, stories, etc.).
   This will allow the individual to "sit at the feet" of others who have a greater knowledge. *"As iron sharpens iron, so does one man sharpen another"* (Proverbs 27:17 NIV). (Always make sure to not blindly accept everything you read, but make certain it is scriptural.)

D) Teach a variety of classes (different age groups, topics, texts).
   When one teaches at many different levels, they become more versatile in their instruction. The more flexibility a teacher has, the more people he will be able to reach out with the life-changing word.

E) Consistently share your recent discoveries with others.
   Reach out to others with your gift of Teaching to share your discoveries with each other. They will be able to further sharpen you and vice-versa. This also allows you to open your thoughts up to scrutiny, which in return tests whether or not what you learned is true.

F) Go to seminars whenever possible.
   This will allow the individual the ability to begin specializing in particular areas of interest. As one matures over the years, it is necessary to hone their focus of learning - and possibly become an expert in a field of study.

Wonderful Webster

Webster grew up in the church and became a Christian when a teenager. As often happens with youth, as he started to enter his adult years, he drifted away and ended up living a life of rebellion towards God. He joined the military and was further nurtured in the ways of the world. By his thirties, he was married and living on the opposite side of the country from his family. As time passed, he began to think back to his roots in Christ and reconsider his present path in life.

In the summer of 2014, Webster made a trip back to his hometown to visit his parents. Though I met him a number of years back, this was the first time that I was able to spend any time with him. He had an interest in being restored to Jesus and wanted to visit with me. That afternoon, we had a great time together discussing the Scriptures. I could recognize almost immediately that he had the passion of a Teacher by his willingness to ask deep questions about the Word. And yes, he recommitted his life to Christ.

He became a faithful member in a small, local congregation on the West Coast and I keep in touch with him on a regular basis. In one of our conversations, he went into detail concerning his study habits. He would arise early in the morning to study the Word in great detail and watch some of our recorded Bible lessons online. He was so thrilled to dig into the Bible and discuss the results of his discoveries. It is always wonderful to see someone taking possession of their Spiritual Gift. He is a FLAMING Teacher, devouring everything he comes across.

When I find an incredibly passionate Teacher like Webster, I press them to reach their full potential. They must set their goals high and long-range. I let him know of my intention to take him on a mission trip when the time was right and his education was more advanced. His reaction was one of excitement! At that point, I shared with him a challenging online program through SIBI which would allow him to receive his Bachelor's Degree in Ministry. Within a day, he was registered and taking the first course.

I received a text from Webster the following week. It was with the true passion of a Teacher that he said the following:

"Howdy! I wanted to drop you a line and say.......Thank you.......
Really, thank you. This school work is....well....work! And I love
it! I am being pushed to learn in a way I haven't done in a long
time. Each course, as I look forward, will challenge me and
educate me tremendously. I thank you from the bottom of my
heart for having faith in me and leading me in this direction."

Where will the Lord take him now that he is restored and
empowered in his giftedness? I am persuaded it will be the full-
time ministry, the mission fields of the world, and most of all a
joyous trip to the throne of God on that glorious day!

Chapter Eight

The Gift of
Shepherding

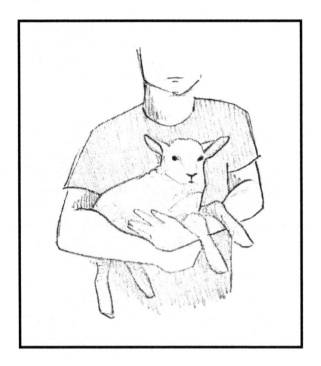

Shepherding Gift – The Passion of Nurturing

Ephesians 4:11, "And He gave some {as} apostles, and some {as} prophets, and some {as} evangelists, and some {as} <u>pastors and teachers</u>…"

The Greek word for shepherd is poimen, meaning "one who takes care of a flock of sheep." The person with the passion of Shepherding is one who deeply desires to lead the flock. They possess vision, patience, guidance, appeal, and care for the sheep. On average, about 16% of a congregation has this as their primary passion.

One must not confuse the office of the shepherd with the Spiritual Gift of Shepherding. The foremost is in regard to the assigned responsibility of certain men leading within the church

(1 Timothy 3:1-7 and Titus 1:5-8). A man or woman who has the inner drive of a Shepherd deeply desires to take care of the flock (church). There is no better example from the Bible of this passion than our Lord and Savior Jesus Christ.

Jesus Had the True Passion of a Shepherd
- Matthew 2:6, *"And you, Bethlehem, land of Judah, are by no means least among the leaders of Judah; for out of you shall come forth a Ruler, who will shepherd My people Israel."* It was for this reason He came into the world!
- John 10:11, *"I am the good shepherd; the good shepherd lays down His life for the sheep."* Jesus was not only willing to lay down His life for the sheep but actually did so on the cross of Calvary!
- Hebrews 13:20, *"Now the God of peace, who brought up from the dead the great Shepherd of the sheep through the blood of the eternal covenant, {even} Jesus our Lord..."* He takes care of His flock in this life and in the life to come!
- 1 Peter 2:25, *"For you were continually straying like sheep, but now you have returned to the Shepherd and Guardian of your souls."* His passion to shepherd is deep to the level of the soul!
- 1 Peter 5:4, *"And when the Chief Shepherd appears, you will receive the unfading crown of glory."* Our Shepherd desires to bestow upon His flock all the glory which God affords us!
- Revelation 7:17, *"...for the Lamb in the center of the throne shall be their shepherd, and shall guide them to springs of the water of life..."* He is not only the Shepherd, but He also fluently speaks the language of "sheep." He will guide us to eternity in heaven with God.

Who are the Shepherds? Though they are not to be confused with the elders of the congregation, they do share many of the same qualities. Those with the gift of nurturing deeply desire to be leaders among the sheep. They tend to do so by being *"...examples to the flock"* (1 Peter 5:3), guiding the younger, more vulnerable Christians as they strive to find their way in Christ.

Being a gospel minister, I often do not have the time to follow-up with every convert for the long term. I will connect them to the loving arms of the members who have the passion of a Shepherd, knowing that the new converts will be nurtured and encouraged to maturity.

Jesus illustrated the characteristics of Shepherding while instructing Peter in John 21:15-17, *"Feed my lambs... Feed my sheep... Feed my sheep."* The point of the passage was to make sure Peter would demonstrate his love for Jesus by taking care of the people of God. Let's face it - newborn lambs must be nurtured in the ways of God. The Spiritual Gift of Shepherding is the drive needed to take the young, vulnerable lamb to the point of full grown ram.

David wrote, in reflection of God being a Shepherd, *"He makes me lie down in green pastures; He leads me beside quiet waters"* (Psalm 23:2). Paul spoke to the elders of Ephesus in Acts 20:28 and warned them to, *"Be on guard for yourselves and for all the flock, among which the Holy Spirit has made you overseers, to shepherd the church of God which He purchased with His own blood."* Concerning the passion of the Shepherd, there is a burning need to protect and provide for the flock. If this passion is not properly employed in the congregation, many can be lost to the ravenous wolves of the world (sin, doubt, despair and false teachers).

Signs of Maturity
    1)   They are Protective.
        A) They guard against wolves.

There is a real danger from outside the church family. The *"savage wolves"* (Acts 20:29) of the world desire to infiltrate the church family and destroy lives. With a mature Shepherd on duty, it likely won't happen.

B)   They guard against "false sheep."

Jesus warned His people about *"false prophets, who come to you in sheep's clothing"* (Matthew 7:15). Often the most dangerous attacks against the church arise from within. The mature Shepherd is highly sensitive to infighting and petty garbage that can appear in the church. They will move quickly to deal with it.

C)   They guard against the *"roaring lion."*

Peter warned the Christians in 1 Peter 5:8 to *"Be of sober {spirit,} be on the alert. Your adversary, the devil, prowls about like a roaring lion, seeking someone to devour."* The devil ultimately wants to kill off the sheep one by one from a congregation. The individual with the emotions of the Shepherd knows this and is willing to actively guard against it.

Don't Mess With The Sheep!

Sister White tested highest on the Shepherd category when we first held classes in our congregation. It should have been no surprise to me since she headed the Human Rights Commission for Pennsylvania, a position which dealt with fair treatment of minorities. It was a dream job for a Shepherd.

There have been a number of times I witnessed her gift of Shepherding on display in her life, but none more apparent than an incident in 2004. Our congregation was dealing with a matter of discipline, and the church family was asked to confront an erring brother (Matthew 18:15-18). We needed to immediately make some last ditch efforts to lead him back to Christ (James 5:19-20). The whole issue generated some disharmony in the church family, which caused great stress in the heart of Sister White.

Being the passionate Shepherd she is, Sister White called a meeting of the elders, wanting to make sure that everything was being done to bring back the brother from the error of his ways. Normally she is a quiet, reserved lady, but that evening Sister White was in rescue mode. She wanted to know that all attempts had been made to *snatch him out of the fire* (Jude 1:23). It wasn't until she was brought up to date on the many months of futile efforts that Sister White was able to find resolution.

It is so difficult for a Shepherd to give up on someone. They will go to the ends of the earth to keep an erring Christian from going the way of the world. The Shepherd's passion is a powerful force which guides them on a quest of recovery. They want to be able to call together their friends and neighbors, saying, *"Rejoice with me, for I have found my sheep which was lost!"* (Luke 15:6).

Knowing of Sister White's gift, I would often encourage her to reach out to the single ladies of our congregation to offer guidance. One in particular was a young Christian woman from West Africa. She was struggling with some deep issues which needed to be addressed by the elders. Knowing the dynamic of the meeting would be awkward (four men and a single woman), I asked Sister White to be with the young lady. It not only changed the climate of the conference but led to resolution of the conflict. Had she not been there, the meeting could very well have ended in disaster and misunderstanding.

We Must Employ the Shepherds.

Too many times we do not use the Spiritual Gifts that God has placed in the body of Christ. There are many inactive Christians just waiting to fulfill a meaningful, functional ministry, but they are relegated to the sidelines of irrelevance. Everyone, including the Shepherds, has a role to fulfill.

2) <u>They are Patient.</u>
    A) They are willing to wait for growth.

    The mature perspective of the Shepherd knows that it could take many years to bring a Christian to fullness (Ephesians 4:13). They do not rush the process but wait patiently for the fruits of a mature Christian (Luke 13:6-9).

    B) They are willing to wait for punishment.

    The established Shepherd knows the natural consequences of God will more than likely better teach than the applied penalties of another person. They have seen it happen many times in the past and will be there to help the younger Christian recover.

    C) They are willing to wait for rescue.

    One of the best traits of the mature Shepherd is the ability to time the rescue when the sheep are in danger. Often the worst thing to do for an erring Christian is to turn the "pig pen" (Luke 15:15) into a penthouse through early rescue. They allow the young lamb to "come to his senses" (Luke 15:17), which then leads to restoration.

<u>Living in a House Divided</u>

Often when there is a split in a congregation, there is division among the giftedness of the group. While holding the seminar for a congregation in Arizona, I discovered this during an evaluation of the departing group in a church split. When the testing was complete, it was revealed that the departing members of the congregation were primarily Encouragers, Mercy Givers, Servants, and Shepherds.

A further investigation exposed that their split had to do with the mistreatment of others at the hands of the Teachers, Prophets, and Evangelists from the other group. They simply did not understand how different they were in pursuit of the same heavenly goal. Had all of them known and appreciated the diversity of their Spiritual Giftedness, they likely would still be together today. Imagine what would have happened had a couple of mature Shepherds nurtured them in such a way. Unfortunately, we will never know what could have been, and now there are *two* dysfunctional congregations in that city, each heavily weighted toward one grouping of Spiritual Giftedness – not a recipe for success.

3) They are Personal.
   A) They know the flock.
      Mature Shepherds know their flock very well, for that is of high importance to them. They know that effectiveness is based in nurturing relationships forged in the lives of others.

   B) They tend the flock.
      When there is a need, the mature Shepherd moves to action every time. If someone is down, then the Shepherd encourages. If someone is suffering from physical needs, they are there to provide assistance. If one's spiritual life is a wreck, Shepherds feel the need to intervene.

   C) They unite the flock.
      The one with a true passion of nurturing seeks above all to have unification of the flock. They know a united and happy congregation is a church which pleases Christ.

Brother Bob

For many decades Bob Williams was not only an elder at the Camp Hill Church of Christ, he was also an extreme Shepherd. Harmony within the body of Christ was the most important priority to him. The best phrase to describe Bob was "team player." If there was a preacher/elder's meeting, he was there. If there was a small–group, home Bible study, he would participate. If I needed someone to go with me on a home visit, he was always available.

The same participation was witnessed on the mission fields of Ghana where Bob was a full-time missionary for three years. He made more than thirty other mission trips to Kumasi, Ghana in order to nurture the new converts of that country.

When I was first hired at Camp Hill, he felt it prudent to further develop my skills by taking me along on some of his trips. While in Ghana, I taught at the Ghana Bible College and participated in some gospel campaigns in the Western Region. I saw firsthand his incredible passion of Shepherding.

Many times following a worship service in one of the congregations in "the bush," the leaders of the church would call on him to resolve some of the conflicts among the congregation. Instead of taking another to court (1 Corinthians 6:1), they would seat him in a judgment chair and bring the two parties before him. He would hear the case and render a decision. Because they respected his age (mid-seventies), his leadership skills (an elder), and mostly his ability to listen (Spiritual Gift of Shepherding), whatever decision he would render would be accepted. Their admiration for him was great because they recognized his passion as a nurturer. He was one of the finest Christian men I have ever known.

A few years later his health began to fade. One Sunday morning he failed to show up for worship. We received a call that an ambulance had been dispatched to his home. About twenty of the members went up to the hospital to discover that Bob had suffered a massive heart attack. There we were, gathered around his bed, watching the vitals drop before our eyes and wanting him not to die. We held hands, sang hymns, and offered prayers, but it was evident that he would be gone in a few minutes. As we said one final prayer, a doctor friend from

Ghana pronounced his death.

In retrospect, the passionate Shepherd had gathered the church together one more time – just like he would have wanted. In his life he nurtured the church to be in harmony; in his death he had done the same.

Signs of Immaturity

   1)   <u>They are Independent.</u>

       A)   They tend to be prideful.

           This is because so many depend on them. They actually begin to believe the world is held together through their efforts.

       B)   They tend to be controlling.

           Immature Shepherds often feel their way is the best way. Micro-managing becomes a tool of the trade when this scenario arises.

       C)   They tend to be heroes.

           This is because they are so sacrificial. They end up developing a Messiah complex and feel the need to rescue.

Baaaaaaad Shepherd!

Becky was a lovely Christian who really enjoyed being involved in the congregation. Most would have considered her a core member of the group. She was always there to assist in any of the group activities. But, she was a major Shepherd with big problems as a result of her immaturity.

This was never more apparent than in the lives of her children. Early on, she attempted to micromanage them, bidding to protect them from all dangers of the world. She did not allow them to go to public school lest they be exposed to the "heathens." This worked until they rebelled, experimenting in bad behavior, drugs, and materialism. She was the first to tell others how to be a parent, but she was unwilling to admit her own downfalls. If one ever offered advice on parenting, her response was complete pride and denial. If a teacher or elder of the congregation attempted to encourage her children in the right way, she attacked them in response.

Everything finally caught up with her as the children reached adulthood. They were deep into the world, posting partying photos on Facebook and Twitter, dating and marrying undesirable characters, and forgetting their commitments to God. She had rescued them from the natural consequences for years, and it finally reached a climax. Becky left the church, moved out of state, and is no longer in fellowship with anyone. Her children practice unfaithfulness to this day.

> 2) <u>They are Neglectful.</u>
>   A) They tend to neglect their spouse.
>   B) They tend to neglect their children.
>   C) They tend to neglect themselves.

One of the areas the immature Shepherd can go astray is in *their* primary flock, the family. It always breaks my heart to see neglect by them at the cost of their loved ones. Young Shepherds must quickly learn to incorporate their household into the church instead of imposing the church on the family.

<u>Don't Forget to Lead Your Own Flock.</u>
I met a man from a congregation in the Midwest who attended one of the Spiritual Giftedness seminars. He had taken the course and confirmed that his Spiritual Gift was highest in Shepherd. In visiting with him over lunch, I was able to know him a bit better and discovered his family life was a wreck. Though he had been a Christian for many years, his wife and three children had all turned their backs on Christ.

Further investigation revealed that he was not a mature Christian and his shortcomings were largely responsible for a track record of neglect. He had been heavily involved in the ministries of the church, but he failed to make his own family his first ministry.

Paul said in Ephesians 5:33, *"Nevertheless, each individual among you also is to love his own wife even as himself, and the wife must see to it that she respects her husband."* He further instructed in Ephesians 6:4, *"Fathers, do not provoke your children to anger, but bring them up in the discipline and instruction of the Lord."* This man neglected that responsibility for years, and it resulted in him attending worship services alone.

Knowing your spiritual gifts can prevent so much damage to the ones we love most. He would have given anything to have matured for the sake of his own family, but it was too late.

3) <u>They become Discouraged.</u>
   A) They tend to overwork the flock.

   The Shepherd must understand the necessity to not overwork the sheep of the flock in their efforts to aid personal growth. If they fail to adjust, then burnout will result.

   B) They tend to be overly patient.

   There is a story of a youth minister who pulled into a rural gas station. He asked the attendant if he had seen a church bus filled with youth. The attendant answered, "Yes, they came by about fifteen minutes ago." The youth minister responded, "Thanks! I am their leader and need to catch up."

   Sometimes the sheep might outrun the Shepherd, forcing them into a game of catch up. When that happens, an immature Shepherd might tire out and give up. Encourage them to press on when applicable.

   C) They tend to be unrealistic.

   Their goals are set too high for newbies in Christ. They must realize that they were also newborn lambs in need of realistic goals. Do not expect a newborn lamb to catch up with the older, mature sheep.

The Driver of the Sheep

Gene was a very talented but immature Shepherd in a small congregation. He was outgoing and heavily involved with those in the church. The difficulty came for Gene when people were not living up to his personal expectations, which frustrated him greatly. His inexperience led him to the solution of doubling down on others who were not growing at the rate he deemed appropriate. This drove many people away because it came across as overbearing. They simply could not see the truth because the message was blurred in the backdrop of an adrenaline-driven Shepherd. They were irritated by this, saying, "Whatever I do is not good enough!" He was not a Shepherd to the sheep, but a driver to the butcher.

Things did not go well for Brother Gene in the end, for his wife left him, his children no longer spoke to him, and he gave up on God. If he would have only matured his gift, this would have made all the difference in the end. If it is God's goal for our *joy to be full*, then Gene fell flat in his spiritual gifts.

Some ways to obtain joy with this gift.

    A)   Start a "New Christians" class.

This is a natural for the one with the Spiritual Giftedness of Shepherd. They want to invest in others to encourage growth and spiritual development.

    B)   Make regular visits to dropouts, backsliders, shut-ins, and young Christians.

Shepherds love to emphasize the concept of the church family to others who cannot see the big picture.

C)   Develop strategies to involve members of the church in
     activities.
     Make calls, visit people in their homes, and carry out
     hospital visits. These are all necessary nutrients in the
     life of a growing Christian.

D)   Participate in, or lead, one-on-one studies with
     Christians.
     There can be no grounding if the new converts do not
     dwell in the Word of God. The Shepherd is willing to
     follow-up with a long-term goal in mind.

E)   Be a defender of the weak, protecting those who do not
     or cannot defend themselves.
     When someone is being bullied within or without the
     congregation, connect them to one with the passion of
     the Shepherd. They will protect!

F)   Teach a class on Spiritual Giftedness for the equipping
     of the saints.
     Shepherds tend to love this tool in their hands because
     it develops mature and effective Christians. Watching
     others discover and employ their gifts will bring joy to
     the Shepherd's heart.

Sheep on a Mountain

During my last trip to Romania, we spent a day atop a
beautiful mountain overlooking many castles below. It was a
wonderful relief from the hot summer air. While sitting with
another missionary, I could hear the sound of many sheep at a
lower elevation, but could see only big boulders on the ground.
The other missionary asked me if I could hear sheep in the
background, to which I could, yet neither of us could see a single
one.

All of a sudden, a man appeared from behind a big rock from below. He began walking over the ridge of the mountain. The man turned back and made a loud noise as if calling out to someone. Immediately the many gray boulders on the mountainside stood up and began walking toward him. They were the sheep we could hear, but could not see. They were following their shepherd to different pastures.

I instantly thought of John 10:14, *"I am the good shepherd; and I know My own, and My own know Me."* Those sheep knew and trusted their leader to guide them in their daily living. They knew his voice because he had spent countless hours nurturing them along the way.

We must not only find the people in the congregation who have a burning passion to Shepherd, but employ them in the ministry for Christ. They have the hunger to lead others to the *green pastures* and *still waters* of God (Psalm 23:2), if only we empower them.

Chapter Nine

The Gift of Encouragement

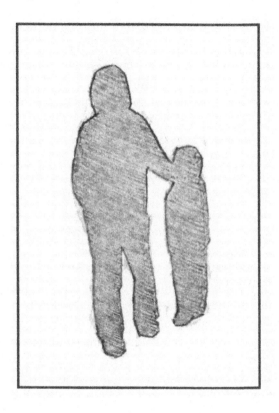

Exhortation – The Passion of Encouragement (Romans 12:8)

Romans 12:8, *"...or he who exhorts, in his exhortation..."*

Typically, about 7% of a congregation will be highest in this gift. The Greek word used for exhortation is parakaleo. Para [near or beside] + kaleo [to call]. Together, the words mean "to call beside or near."

In Luke 16:25, we find this word in its purest form, *"But Abraham said, 'Child, remember that during your life you received your good things, and likewise Lazarus bad things; but now he is being <u>comforted</u> here, and you are in agony.'"* Abraham was closely holding Lazarus, and it was called *"comforted."* It communicated the concept of acceptance with encouragement.

The closest identifiable action which I liken to parakaleo is one person extending to another the offer of an embracing hug, calling them to acceptance. This is why the word is often translated *"comfort"* in the Bible.

It is similar to what transpired with Barnabas in the life of the Apostle Paul as he first attempted to meet with the other apostles in Jerusalem. It says in Acts 9:26-27, *"And when he had come to Jerusalem, he was trying to associate with the disciples; and they were all afraid of him, not believing that he was a disciple. But Barnabas took hold of him and brought him to the apostles and described to them how he had seen the Lord on the road, and that He had talked to him, and how at Damascus he had spoken out boldly in the name of Jesus."*

The Encourager is a person who strives to be incredibly welcoming to those around them, helping maintain a spirit of congeniality in the congregation. They absolutely love to lift the hearts, souls, and minds of others to a level of great happiness. They deeply desire to have an environment of unified Christians, living in harmony in the Lord. The Encourager wants to "put courage in" the souls of others. They need to lift the spirits of others who might be going through a tough time, so as to cause that person to glorify God in the end.

Some Encouragers Mentioned in the Bible
Barnabas was an Encourager.
- Acts 4:36-37, *"And Joseph, a Levite of Cyprian birth, who was also called Barnabas by the apostles (which translated means, Son of Encouragement), and who owned a tract of land, sold it and brought the money and laid it at the apostles' feet."*
- Acts 11:22-23, *"And the news about them reached the ears of the church at Jerusalem, and they sent Barnabas off to Antioch. Then when he had come and witnessed the grace of God, he rejoiced and {began} to encourage them all with resolute heart to remain {true} to the Lord."*

[Note: Encouragement was the primary Spiritual Gift of Barnabas. It is not only important to know the primary gift of an individual, but also the secondary and tertiary gifts. It typically points to the how the primary will be carried out in the life of the person. In the case of Barnabas, it was through the actions of Giving and Missions.]

Judas and Silas were Encouragers.
- Acts 15:30-32, *"So, when they were sent away, they went down to Antioch; and having gathered the congregation together, they delivered the letter. And when they had read it, they rejoiced because of its encouragement. And Judas and Silas ...encouraged and strengthened the brethren with a lengthy message."*

John the Baptist was an Encourager.
- Luke 3:18, *"So with many other exhortations also he preached the gospel to the people."* People often hold the perspective of John the Baptist as an "in your face" spokesman for God, but here we find him as an encourager of the people.

Paul was an Encourager.
- 1 Thessalonians 2:11, *"...just as you know how we {were} exhorting and encouraging and imploring each one of you as a father {would} his own children..."* Paul put courage in the hearts of the Thessalonian Christians through his teachings and actions.

Paul also received encouragement back from other Christians.
- Colossians 4:10-11, *"Aristarchus, my fellow prisoner, sends you his greetings; and {also} Barnabas's cousin Mark (about whom you received instructions; if he comes to you, welcome him); and {also} Jesus who is called Justus; these are the only fellow workers for the kingdom*

> *of God who are from the circumcision, and they have proved to be an encouragement to me."*

God, Jesus, and the Holy Spirit are all considered Encouragers or comforters.

- The Father - 2 Corinthians 1:3-7, *"Blessed {be} the God and Father of our Lord Jesus Christ, the Father of mercies and God of all <u>comfort</u>, who <u>comforts</u> us in all our affliction so that we may be able to <u>comfort</u> those who are in any affliction with the <u>comfort</u> with which we ourselves are <u>comforted</u> by God. For just as the sufferings of Christ are ours in abundance, so also our <u>comfort</u> is abundant through Christ. But if we are afflicted, it is for your <u>comfort</u> and salvation; or if we are <u>comforted</u>, it is for your <u>comfort</u>, which is effective in the patient enduring of the same sufferings which we also suffer; and our hope for you is firmly grounded, knowing that as you are sharers of our sufferings, so also you are {sharers} of our <u>comfort</u>."*

[Note: In this passage Paul uses *parakaleo* ten times to prove God as the source of all comfort. He is the origin of comfort, imparting it unto us though Christ Jesus with the intent for us to pass it on to others who are suffering.]

- The Son - Matthew 11:28-30, *"Come to Me, all who are weary and heavy-laden, and I will give you rest. Take My yoke upon you and learn from Me, for I am gentle and humble in heart, and you will find rest for your souls. For My yoke is easy and My burden is light."* Jesus appealed to all mankind to place their burdens upon Him. He was placing encouragement in the lives of others with the intent of comfort.
- The Holy Spirit - John 14:16, *"And I will pray the Father, and he shall give you another <u>Comforter</u>, that he may*

abide with you forever..." John 14:26, "*But the <u>Comforter</u>, which is the Holy Ghost, whom the Father will send in my name, he shall teach you all things, and bring all things to your remembrance, whatsoever I have said unto you.*" John 15:26, "*But when the <u>Comforter</u> is come, whom I will send unto you from the Father, even the Spirit of truth, which proceedeth from the Father, he shall testify of me...*" John 16:7, "*Nevertheless I tell you the truth; It is expedient for you that I go away: for if I go not away, the <u>Comforter</u> will not come unto you; but if I depart, I will send him unto you.*"

[Note: The King James Version actually uses the term "Comforter" for the Holy Spirit.]

<u>The Primary Message of Encouragement: Salvation with Jesus!</u>
- 1 Thessalonians 4:16-18, "*For the Lord Himself will descend from heaven with a shout, with the voice of {the} archangel, and with the trumpet of God, and the dead in Christ shall rise first. Then we who are alive and remain shall be caught up together with them in the clouds to meet the Lord in the air, and thus we shall always be with the Lord. Therefore comfort one another with these words.*" Reminding others of the coming resurrection and eternal life is the most encouraging message for the struggling Christians in their times of need.

Signs of Maturity
1) Their *Attitude.*
   A) They are self-driven.
   B) They are optimists.
   C) They are motivators.

The mature Encourager is the most uplifting individual one can find in life. For them the glass is always half-full and never half-empty. They hold a positive attitude in all circumstances, both good and bad, usually causing others to develop an optimistic attitude as well.

<u>Lovely Lois</u>

Lois was a long-time Christian and one of the greatest Encouragers I ever had the honor of meeting. She always displayed a smile on her face and a warm handshake or hug for everyone she greeted. I met her while interviewing for a congregation many years ago. She came up to me after worship, thanking me for the lesson, and encouraging me to further pursue the opportunities there. She struck me as someone who did not have a care in the world.

Later I went to lunch with some of the other members of the congregation. I remarked to one of them about Lois and how welcoming she was to me. It was then I learned of the devastating health issues of this sister. One of the brothers told me that she was suffering from her third bout of cancer. She had endured countless chemotherapy treatments and surgeries through that time. For years, she fought a daily battle just to make it to the next day, but her heart of Encouragement concealed it all. She was determined to not hamper the spirits of anyone.

I was hired at that congregation, and sadly, Lois continued to have health issues. During some of my hospital visits to her, I would look into the room to find her in pain or sick to her stomach. Upon seeing me, she would immediately radiate a smile. [Note: This is one of the major signs of the Encourager, being able to quickly shift from a sad look to a beaming smile when someone else comes into their presence. They are so determined to brighten your day. A smile is one of the greatest tools in their arsenal.]

Lois always brought out the best in those around her, even in the depths of her sickness. The nurses and doctors really appreciated her. They mentioned to me that they would often go into her room to be cheered up when they were having a rough day. It was the consensus among them that she was still alive, not because of their great skills, but because of her positive spirit. Indeed they were correct, for Lois lived until the age of sixty-nine, nearly two-decades into battle with the cancer that eventually took her home to the arms of Jesus. She might be gone now, but her passion of Encouragement lives on in the hearts of the lives she touched.

    2)   They are *Expressive.*
        A)   They are creative.
        B)   They are communicators.
        C)   They are practical.

The mature Encouragers are very expressive in how they interact with others. Their creativity is demonstrated in the cards they make, the letters they write, and the words they speak. They love to make visits more than those of the other Spiritual Gifts. They are very practical in their relationships, often willing to be there when the times are tough.

The Young Encourager with the Well-Aged Passion

I say with confidence that the greatest Encourager whom I have known is my youngest daughter, Abbie. My wife and I noticed this from the time she could walk and talk. Abbie would stand near the fireplace and re-enact scenes from the television show *Barney and Friends*, trying to put a smile on our faces. When we would laugh, the joy in her heart was evident. Abbie knew she had done well to cause us to forget any possible cares of the day.

As she grew, so did her drive for Encouragement. When her friends would come for a sleepover, it was Abbie who assumed the role of an activities director, planning the events of the night to keep them entertained. On those evenings, the laughter of her friends permeated our home as she kept them in her grip of humor.

Through elementary and high school, her passion fully blossomed. When permitted, Encouragers like to be involved in many activities. With Abbie, we could barely keep up with her. She was active in JROTC, Future Farmers of America, Cumberland Valley Television, soccer, water polo, softball, volleyball, mentoring programs, Special Olympics, orphanages, nursing home ministries, children's ministries, mission trips, Bible camps, and youth groups. She was even a Dairy Princess (although in reality mildly lactose intolerant). As one might expect from a flaming Encourager, she was the 2013 Pennsylvania Miss Congeniality. Why all these activities? These activities gave her the opportunity to talk to others about Christ.

Abbie is always making cards for the sick and deeply longs to go on visits to shut-ins. Many of these individuals keep the cards because they were made with such creativity and personal love. She enjoys making nursing home visits, knowing their need is *"light for a dark day"* (2 Peter 1:19).

I am persuaded that the Lord will always bless the person who fervently follows their ministerial passion. With Abbie, this reality once again proved to be true. All those activities, connections, and faith-building relationships not only broadened her possibilities in Christ, but won her a full-tuition scholarship for Christian service to Abilene Christian University. Although Abbie is young physically, in her passion of Encouragement, she is well-aged. I am excited to see where the Lord takes her in this life.

   3) They have healthy *Relationships.*
      A) They are unifiers.
      B) They are friendly.
      C) They are counselors.

A mature Encourager utilizes their gift to demonstrate friendliness to produce unity in the body of Christ. Their sociability often wins people over to a new perspective. Encouragers are counselors in the sense that they want others who are disheartened to gain a new lease on life. They are the cohesive glue which holds the congregation together in the midst of crisis.

The Radiant Encourager

Becky was one of the first Christians I met in what became my first church home. She was heavily involved in the children's ministry and the toddlers loved her very much. She was middle-aged, had beautiful blue eyes, and a smile that was absolutely contagious. Whenever the young children would come into the church building for Bible class, they would run into her arms, being greeted with a warm hug of acceptance. Becky had all the attributes of an extreme Encourager.

Sometimes, immature Christians might want to sleep in on a Sunday morning instead of going to worship services. There was a period in my first year as a Christian when I missed worship three weeks in a row. Nobody reached out to contact me, and I felt forgotten.

Just when I started to feel insignificant in the congregation and was on the verge of venturing into dangerous territory, the phone rang. It was Becky. She let me know that she really appreciated me and missed my presence in church. She wanted to make sure everything was okay. I confessed that laziness was the reason and my intention to be in worship that Sunday. I felt guilty because she enjoyed having me in the fellowship and my neglect was hampering her joy.

The next day she invited me to a meal at her house with some other church members. There at her table I was able to connect with other Christians from my age group, some of whom are still my friends to this day. Becky orchestrated a unity among us that made a difference in my life. It caused me to feel accepted and pointed me in the right way. I do not think she was even aware of the impact her gift of Encouragement made in my life.

Signs of Immaturity
1) They are *Impulsive.*
   A)   They tend to interrupt people.
   B)   They tend to act without thinking.
   C)   They tend to move too fast in big decisions.

The impulsiveness of the immature Encourager has led many down the wrong path. Their risky spontaneity is the sure sign they need growth in this area. Interruptions in conversations are a sign they desperately want to connect. Their swift action without proper thought leaves them vulnerable. Their positive outlook can be deceiving in light of the contrary evidence.

The Discouraged Encourager
While teaching this course at a school of preaching in Africa, I came across a student who tested highest in Encourager. Since student preachers tend to be Evangelist and Teachers, I decided to learn more about his ambitions in the ministry.

We had a meal together and conversed about his faith, family, and congregational aspirations. He had an extremely positive outlook on his plans. He planned to return back to his village following graduation and win them all to Christ! I was excited to hear about it and inquired more about the details.

When probing a bit deeper concerning finances, I found his strategy to be lacking considerably. Often in the rural churches of Africa, it is necessary for a preacher to work at least one secular job while building up the church. My concern was for his ability to take care of his wife and four children on such a meager salary.

This brother heard me, but did not listen. He dismissed my concern through proclamation of positive thinking. When I went into the details of a responsible plan, he kept saying, "When the brethren in the U.S. hear about my work, they will want to support it." I was very apprehensive and believed this would place his family in further poverty. I had done my best to dissuade him and felt the natural consequences of his actions would prevail.

He graduated and went back to his village to work full-time in missions. He sent out emails to solicit outside support, but the help never came because the mission was not a well-established work. His congregation could only pay him about half of what he needed and his family began to suffer economically. On another visit to the area about a year later, I found his family in utter poverty. I funded him a one-time gift to bring him back on track and had a long talk with him about better planning. He agreed that he had jumped into the full-time ministry too quickly and would attempt to make wiser decisions in the future.

In the end, he continued his impulsive ways and went even further into deficiency. His positive attitude did not make up for his unrealistic plans for full-time work there. His wife took the children and went back to her home village to live with her parents. The brother dropped out of the ministry, moved away, and is working a secular job in a foreign country. He lost his congregation, his wife, his children, and ultimately his joy. He had an immature gift of Encouragement, and its fruit was destruction.

 2)   They have unstable *Emotions.*
   A)   They are prone to depression.
   B)   They are prone to be unrealistic.
   C)   They are prone to be over-humorous.

This may seem odd concerning the Encourager, but immaturity in this gift often leads to depression. The reason for this is because in their efforts to keep all those around them in a positive mindset, they fail to be encouraged themselves. Immature Encouragers also tend to ignore the realities of serious situations which arise, pushing them off by just trying to think positively. One of the ways they do this is to "laugh it off" or by being inappropriately humorous.

The Depressed Encourager
Sister Lynn was a passionate Encourager who strove in her love to uplift others. Her greatest joy in life was to make people

feel great about themselves. If someone stopped over at her home, it meant a long visit. She would make many visits to the shut-ins of the church. She craved fellowship and exercised it through her gift.

Though Lynn was sincere about this area of her life, she still had a level of immaturity that needed attention. She could not find the "off button" to her drive. Often her desire to encourage would end up costing her sleep. Many times while at a home for a visit, she would simply doze off in the middle of a conversation. Sometimes she felt so compelled to uplift others that she would actually resist going to sleep for the night in order to prepare a meal, write cards, and make telephone calls.

Her lack of sleep brought on anxiety and then depression. She started losing weight from all of the emotional issues. Lynn simply would not take the time to recharge her "Encouragement battery" when it was running low. Through all that, she still attempted to be the Encourager but produced only concern in the lives of those who loved her. Before it was over, she nearly had a nervous breakdown. Thank God she sought help and received it.

3) They are often *Intense.*
   A)   They may encourage others into actions.
   B)   They may encourage others into inactivity.
   C)   They may encourage others into ignorance.

We must remember Encouragers are by nature non-confrontational. When you add immaturities to the equation, bad things happen. Sometimes there needs to be correction before a person can be encouraged. When the Encourager fails to incorporate this fact, they end up encouraging others in the wrong ways. Immature Encouragers must beware lest they lead people to do the wrong actions.

The Ineffective Encourager
While holding a meeting on the West Coast in 2005, I met a preacher who was extremely low in Evangelism and high in

Encourager. He had been at his congregation for more than a decade, but he was unwilling *"do the work of an Evangelist"* (2 Timothy 4:5).

Instead of using his passion to encourage others to convert through the gospel and personal growth lessons, he decided to take a second secular job of social work for the State of California. He felt it best to find prospects through his secular job and plug them into the work of the church. It sounded great on paper to the congregation, but it was unrealistic because of the secular nature of government.

His congregation dwindled from one hundred members to about twenty during his time there. Many key people left and others were not encouraged to step up. In the end the congregation withered and died. The preacher proved to be an immature Encourager who led his congregation in the wrong ways.

Some Ways to Obtain Joy with This Gift:

A) Write notes of encouragement to others.
   This is a wonderful and effective way to keep others strong in Christ. It could be with emails, letters, or cards.

B) Memorize encouraging verses from the Bible.
   Encouragers love to repeat uplifting statements to the discouraged. Being able to back up those words with the Word of God adds depth to the results.

C) Make many hospital, nursing home, and shut-in visits.
   When encouragers go to a lonely place like this, they shine. Your visit to the forgotten could be the biggest factor to their conversion.

D) Be the one to represent the church family by reaching out to the sick and bereaved.
   If there are flowers to be sent or cards needing to be delivered, give them to the Encouragers. To them it is more than delivery of an arrangement to an address, but the transfer of joy to the heart of the hurting.

E) Develop a close relationship with a couple of others who share the same gift.
Commit to spending time together with other Encouragers. This will allow each other to recharge their enthusiasm.

F) Volunteer at a half-way house, home for troubled teens, or a crisis pregnancy center.
These people are looking for and need guidance in their lives. A mature Encourager is able to successfully steer them in the right direction.

G) Be one of the first to visit the recent dropouts from the congregation.
Dropouts often go the way they do because of a lack of personal relationships. The Encouragers possess the ability and drive to change that.

H) Teach a class on how to be encouraging to others.
Most people in a congregation need to understand how effective Encouragers can be for the work of God. What better teacher could they have for such a task?

Chapter Ten

The Gift of Mercy

Mercy Giver – The Passion of Mercy (Romans 12:8)
Romans 12:8, *"...he who shows mercy, with cheerfulness."*

About 17% of a congregation will test highest in Mercy Giver. The Greek word for mercy is eleos, meaning "one who shows compassion." Jesus said in Matthew 5:7, *"Blessed are the merciful, for they shall receive mercy."* Mercy Givers possess the ability to stand in another's shoes, feel their suffering, and understand their circumstances.

In Mark 10:46-47, a blind beggar name Bartimaeus *"...was sitting by the road. And when he heard that it was Jesus the Nazarene, he began to cry out and say, 'Jesus, Son of David, have mercy on me!'"* He heard about the compassion of Jesus and His power to miraculously heal the hurting. He called out to Jesus, begging him to stand in his shoes and feel what it was like to be blind. Jesus did have mercy on him and restored his sight.

The Mercy Giver has the gift of being able to understand the suffering of others to the extent that they are compelled to help. To gain a better understanding of the characteristics of a Mercy Giver, let us observe some New Testament examples of this passion.

Tabitha Demonstrated Mercy.
     In Acts 9:36-39, we find a Mercy Giver named Tabitha. She abounded *"...with deeds of kindness and charity, which she continually did."* Who were the recipients of her ministry? She specialized in reaching out to the widows of the community, making them *"tunics and garments."* The widows of the first century were the most wounded group of society. For Tabitha to take on the responsibility of ministering to them was not only a demonstration of her character, but also of the ministerial quality of the Mercy Giver.

The Philippian Jailer Demonstrated Mercy.
     In Acts 16:22-34, Paul and Silas were beaten and thrown in a Philippian jail. With their backs raw from flogging, they were imprisoned and left to rot in a cell. Yet, at midnight they *"...were praying and singing hymns of praise to God."* By the end of the account, the two were preaching the gospel to the jailer, leading to conversion of him and his household. It was during the presentation of the gospel that the hardened jailer ministered to Paul and Silas, *"washing their wounds"* and tending to their hunger. He was demonstrating Mercy to the physically hurting while being ministered to with the gospel of spiritual healing.

A Samaritan Was a Mercy Giver.
     Luke 10:25-37 contains one of the greatest examples of a Mercy Giver in the New Testament. Jesus was asked a question by a *'certain lawyer,'* *"...And who is my neighbor?"* Instead of quoting scriptures and citing proof texts, Jesus simply told a parable about a victim who *"fell among robbers."* The man was

traveling from Jerusalem to Jericho on a dangerous road known for crime. He was *"stripped and beaten, leaving him half dead"* (the Encouragers would rephrase, "Well, at least he is half alive!").

While the man was left for dead in the road, two religious individuals who were to be an example of mercy came by. The first one was a priest and the second a Levite. Surely they would come to the aid of the victim, but they did not. One passed by on the right ride and the other on the left. Perhaps they did not demonstrate mercy because they felt danger lurked in the shadows. Maybe they were in a hurry to reach their destination and did not want to be bothered. Either way, they lacked the passion of Mercy.

Verse 30 says, *"But a certain Samaritan, who was on a journey, came upon him; and when he saw him, he felt compassion."* The Samaritan was already in a hurry for his business trip, but when he saw the wounded man in the middle of the road, *he felt compassion*. He connected his heart to the victim's circumstances. His inner drive of Mercy would not allow himself to continue on until he moved into action to alleviate the suffering.

The passage continued, *"and came to him, and bandaged up his wounds, pouring oil and wine on them and he put him on his own beast, and brought him to an inn, and took care of him. And on the next day he took out two denarii and gave them to the innkeeper and said, 'Take care of him; and whatever more you spend, when I return, I will repay you.'"* The Samaritan felt his pain, and that emotion moved him to begin to alleviate the man's suffering.

The passage concludes with *Jesus asking, "Which of these three do you think proved to be a neighbor to the man who fell into the robbers' hands?' And he said, 'The one who showed mercy toward him.' And Jesus said to him, 'Go and do the same.'"*

Even though a Samaritan was looked upon by the Jewish population as a half-breed cousin, his gift of Mercy shined.

When we empower the Mercy Givers of a congregation, the church shines with the compassion of Jesus.

<u>The Mercy Shoes of Jennifer</u>

Too many times we fail to understand the ministerial passions of others. It is extremely important for others to stand in the spiritual shoes of another. Helping people to see through the passions of others is a healthy practice for the church. The Mercy Giver understands this process better than any other.

Take Jennifer for example. She is one of the most passionate Mercy Givers I've ever had the pleasure of meeting. Her heart is tender for God and His people. She loves taking her daughter to nursing homes and hospital visits. If Jennifer knew of someone who was suffering, she would always be available to minister to their soul. I can honestly say she does not have an ill bone in her body.

Jennifer and her husband David were expecting their second child, a son whom they named David III. They looked forward to having another baby and had begun making all the preparations. Nearing the sixth month of their pregnancy, they lost their son through a miscarriage. The hospital recorded the death as being one day short of a still birth. This meant there would be no death certificate and no legal recognition by the government that he was ever a person. Naturally the parents were devastated, and the church family did their best to reach out to them.

Although a government did not define the baby as a living being, we know better. In speaking to the parents, I proposed an idea for a sermon to be preached on a Sunday morning about a month later. With their permission, I taught a lesson titled "The Wonderful Womb People of God." It addressed the various stages of development of a baby in the womb, including many pre-birth photos. On the PowerPoint presentation and in the notes, I placed the tiny footprints and handprints of a pre-born baby.

Some members of the congregation had terrified looks on their faces as I systematically showed the development of a baby in the womb. I heard the mumbling of brothers and sisters in

Christ, "How can this preacher be so insensitive! How dare he do something like this?" What they thought was insensitive and cruel was a well-calculated plan to mimic the experience of a Mercy Giver. Right at about the time the congregation's emotions reached their boiling point, I revealed three reasons for doing the lesson:

1. I desired to prove from the Scriptures that unborn children are people in the eyes of God despite what the secular abortionists proclaim. I did not want a single person in attendance to pretend otherwise.
2. I wished for all the non-Mercy Givers to stand in the shoes of Jennifer, to feel what she did. They needed to better understanding the passion of Mercy in order to best minister to her in the many months to come.
3. I wanted to commemorate the life of David Marrs III in the funeral he never had. The lesson closed with these exact words...

"About one month ago, on October 28th, 2011, Dave and Jennifer Marrs lost their unborn son, David Marrs III, due to complications of pregnancy. The handprints and footprints at the top of the screen are his. They were taken by the nurse at the hospital shortly after his passing. They are a reminder to us that life is fragile and priceless.

Understandably it was a devastating ordeal for them on many levels, but mostly because their dreams for sharing a life with this child are over. In a matter of hours, the joyful anticipation of having a new baby boy turned into the sad event of losing an unborn son. Our hearts go out to the Marrs family in their loss. May young David's soul rest in peace, joy, and happiness forever."

By the end of the sermon, there was not a dry eye in the building. The congregation further valued the life of the unborn;

they stood in the footsteps of a Mercy Giver; they memorialized a child never known. The result was a better trained congregation, understanding fully the heart of a suffering Mercy Giver. For a moment they stood in the shoes of another and were able to better understand. The Marrs family was recently blessed with another son. God is good!

Signs of Maturity
    1)   They have a positive *Attitude.*
        A) They are forgiving in relationships.
        B) They are content in character.
        C) They are gentle in spirit.

I have found over the years that the mature Mercy Giver is the most forgiving of all the Spiritual Gifts. Not only are they willing to let go, they actually tend to forget the faults of others. They are very content with where they stand in Jesus, knowing the depth of His forgiveness. They can also be some of the gentlest souls in the church, not wanting to resort to anything which would bring hurt and sorrow to another.

The Heart of the Mercy Giver
Back in 2011, our congregation adopted a nursing home as one of our primary ministries. There are many services which we have provided, including building projects, singing, Christmas gifts, worship services, and Bible studies. I believe, however, that the most important thing that we do for the residents is to pay them personal visits.

One loyal visitor to the nursing home, who stands out to me as a compassionate Mercy Giver, is a sister named Denise. One of the residents she "adopted" was Herbert, a man from the inner city with bad lungs and a bad heart. He had no visits for nearly three years and was very lonely. Denise focused on changing that. She faithfully made weekly visits, sometimes lasting hours at a time. She made sure he received the best treatment possible and even brought him some of his favorite foods when his appetite waned in illness.

I also followed up with Herb whenever possible. Denise's patience and love was well-spoken of by him and his face would glow whenever I mentioned her. Once when visiting, I saw a picture of him and Denise on the shelf. On his lap was a beautiful, handmade blanket, fashioned by her own hands. When I asked him about it, he welled up with tears in his eyes and said, "That lady really loves me! She is the salt of the earth!" Her mercy nurtured his heart in a way that made him a more complete person and clearly showed him the love of Christ.

Herb's health continued to decline, but his spirit was continually lifted (2 Corinthians 4:16). Through all of the hospitalizations, Denise was there for him, being a source of compassion. She prayed with him, held his hand, and patiently waited as his life faded from this realm. She even oversaw the arrangements at the funeral home, making sure it was handled with honor. Denise carried out Mercy Giving the way Jesus designed for it to be used, because she was active and mature in her gift.

    2)   They have a heart for *Others.*
        A)   They are magnets for the wounded.
        B)   They are listeners for the neglected.
        C)   They are faithful in relationships.

When Mercy Givers are matured, they are incredible magnets to draw the hurting into the church in search of refuge from a cruel world. They listen well and show incredible faithfulness to even the most forgotten souls on the earth. Watching them use their gift is a positive demonstration for us all.

The Mercy-Giving Elder

At Camp Hill we have had several elders over the years, and I enjoy keeping track of their Spiritual Giftedness. It is important for an eldership to have a diversity of gifts in order to effectively reach out to the flock. An eldership of Teachers, Evangelists, and Prophets typically are not as effective in reaching out to the Servants, Mercy Givers, and Encouragers.

That brings us to Darren, an extreme Mercy Giver and one of our current elders. He tested highest in this category.

He retired from the United States Air Force several years ago and decided to go back to school to train for another career. What was his choice of higher education? Counseling of course, for Mercy Givers make the best counselors. They tend to be good listeners, something that is of the highest priority to the Mercy Giver.

I am lowest in Mercy Giver and, as a result, people tend to shy away from me for counseling. I really do not have the patience to listen the way Darren does. I have noticed over the years that whenever someone from the congregation is going through a bad time, it is to Darren they will turn. He has helped many people with sexual sins, poor marriages, personal conflict, and emotional instability. I shudder to think what it would be like if this brother was not one of our elders. I look forward to seeing how God will use him in the future, and I am confident that his merciful heart will continue to help others to grow in their relationships with Jesus.

  3) They are *Attentive.*
     A) They reach out to the poor.
     B) They reach out to the ill.
     C) They reach out to the aged.

One of the most common phrases a Mercy Giver will hear is, "I don't know where you find these people!" This is because they attract so many of the downtrodden in society. While others in the church family might reach out to many types of people, the mature Mercy Giver focuses on the hurting, the poor, and the forgotten. They are not afraid to take on a prospect who might require more time and patience than average.

The Diamond in the Rough

Samantha was a young convert who I met in my first year in Pennsylvania. She sported a 'buzz cut,' was covered in tattoos, punctured with piercings, and talked tough in her conversations. If you were to see her on the street while driving through town, Samantha's image might lead you to believe you were in a bad neighborhood. She visually blended in with an average congregation like a 1974 Ford Pinto in a Mercedes Benz new car lot.

It is said that one cannot judge a book by its cover. This is true, for Jesus does not judge the appearance of a man, but the content of his heart (John 7:24). In Samantha's case, she might have been a tough looking bruiser on the outside, but on the inside she is a passionate Mercy Giver.

In all the Spiritual Gifts, people will tend to gravitate towards a primary area of focus. Samantha's particular Mercy-Giver passion has been for children - she has always interacted well with them. One of her joys has been working in the kitchen at Bible camp. It is not the fresh air that motivates her to attend, but rather the children she gets to be around.

For my first trip to India, Samantha sent a suitcase full of toys for the kids. They all loved everything that was sent. She really has a merciful heart towards children. Every year that I have known her, she has been a lead volunteer for *Toys for Tots*, an organization that distributes thousands of toys every year to poor children in our area. Samantha has also recruited children from our youth group to assist, making it a doubly-great joy.

As it so happens, the ministry that first drew her into the love of Christ was a Vacation Bible School in 2002. I remember her speaking about the rough life she had and some things parents should avoid when raising children. Where will the Lord take her in the future? Only He knows. One thing is for sure; her endeavors will be driven by the gift of Mercy and will likely involve children.

Signs of Immaturity
   1) They are *Indecisive.*
       A) They are often inconsistent in reactions.
       B) They are often neglectful in corrections.
       C) They are often doormats in relationships.

   When a Mercy Giver has failed to take the time to mature, trouble can be on the horizon. They tend to forgive when they need to discipline. This is because their natural tendency is to avoid conflict. When that pattern is followed, everything begins to fall apart on many levels.

Norma the Doormat
   I have noticed throughout the years that women who are victims of violence tend to be immature Mercy Givers. In Norma's case, this was absolutely true. I met her while teaching a class on Spiritual Giftedness. From some of the things she spoke of, I could tell that she was a wounded soul. Her words also confirmed to me that she was likely a Mercy Giver, for she was being abused and neglected by her husband, yet she continued to forgive. Another clue was her profession. Norma was a registered nurse which is a Mercy Giver's dream job. When she took the written test, it was confirmed that she was a full-blown, four-alarm, immature Mercy Giver.
   As time went on, Norma revealed more information about the abuse she was receiving from her non-Christian husband. Not only would he scream and threaten her, but he would often physically abuse her as well. Norma's husband was also a heroin addict and slept up to eighteen hours a day. I was amazed that a Christian woman would even allow such evil in her life.
   The problem had gotten out of hand over the years because of Norma's unwillingness to confront him at the very beginning. When her husband raised his voice to her, and then sought forgiveness, Norma forgave. When he continued to abuse her,

and then blame her for the abuse, she dismissed it and moved on.

After they had children together, his pressures mounted and he became more belligerent toward her. For the sake of the family, Norma kept silent. Then came the drugs, the beatings, and the cheating. Every time she kept taking him back without holding his feet to the fire.

She confided in me how bad the situation was. In shock about her silent suffering, I encouraged her to confront him about the behavior. When she finally mustered up the strength to do so, he reacted poorly, being unwilling to accept her step of maturation. In the end she took her kids, moved away, and started a new life with a new perspective.

The law of the reaper (Galatians 6:7-8) says that we reap what we sow; we reap more than we sow; and we reap after we sow. Even though she left her past behind, her past caught up to her. One night she answered her front door and was shocked to find her drugged-up ex-husband. She woke up in the hospital, and he woke up in jail. He simply could not emotionally cope with the mature Mercy Giver that Norma had become.

2) They are *Emotional.*
    A) They are prone to depression.
    B) They are prone to sorrow.
    C) They are prone to over-sensitivity.

An immature Mercy Giver tends to be more susceptible to suffering from depression. In their efforts to reach out to the downtrodden, they end up being overwhelmed with the collective sorrow. They tend to have much sorrow in their lives as a result of internally taking on the problems of others. Mercy Givers also tend to be over-sensitive in their reactions to others who confront them.

166 Chapter 10 Spiritual Giftedness
The Ten Spiritual Gifts: The Gift of Mercy

Super-Sensitive Sandy

Sandy was a good friend of our family, but immature in her passion of Mercy. She tended to base things on her feelings and not on the facts of the Bible. She was incredibly emotional in all aspects of her life. If there was a sad movie on television, she would cry for about an hour after it was over. If she saw an injured cat or dog, it would break her heart. If her daughter wanted something, it would tug at Sandy's heart until she gave in. She was too sensitive with her gift of Mercy.

One time during a Bible study, I disagreed with her subjective viewpoints. Being extremely low in Mercy Giver, I attempted to ground her in the objective truth of the Bible. Sandy viewed my correction as an insensitive, personal attack, and I can still hear my wife saying, "You made Sandy cry!" From then on, knowing that Mercy Giving was her highest passion and also my lowest, I made sure to adjust my interactions with her accordingly.

Sandy was diagnosed with cancer a few years later, and I was grateful for this resolution we had reached in our relationship. Our family had moved away and could not visit very often, but as the disease spread and whittled her life away, I was able to regularly call on the phone and be a comfort to her. I fluently spoke her language, and we had a good connection at the end of her life. Sandy died at age forty-four, leaving behind a beautiful daughter.

3) They lack Perspective.
   A) They tend to be uninformed.
   B) They tend to be disorganized.
   C) They tend to be undisciplined.

The subjectivity of the immature Mercy Giver also tends to lead them to be uninformed of the perspective of others. When exercising their Mercy for others, they tend to overlook obvious warning signs that it is time to cut loose an irreparable relationship. They also tend to be disorganized in their logic and undisciplined in their approach to correction.

Broken Brent

Brent was a Christian husband and father as well as an extreme Mercy Giver. Though it had been twenty years since his conversion, he was still a baby in his faith. He refused to mature in his passion, and it led him in the wrong way concerning his family and finances.

His wife, also very high in Mercy Giver, loved to spend money they did not have on things they did not need. Brent felt it best to not say anything because he did not want to hurt her feelings by saying "No." He was a financial doormat. In the first decade of their marriage, they filed for bankruptcy. You think they would have learned their lesson, but about eight years later they filed a second time.

When it came to the three children, the state of affairs was also a disaster. Neither parent would take the time to discipline their kids. They usually ended up being pushed around by them. If his daughters wanted something, they received it, even when it wasn't in the budget. If they wanted to listen to filthy music, date questionable characters, or stay out until all hours of the night, Brent would not confront lest he upset them.

Before it was over, two of the three girls were mothers out of wedlock, unfaithful to God, and living immoral lifestyles. Brent and his wife left their congregation and may have even left the Lord as a result of the misapplication of his gift. The Spiritual Gift of Mercy is good, but only if it is matured.

Some Ways to Obtain Joy with This Gift

A. Seek out and comfort the lonely and the forgotten in a congregation.

In every congregation, there are people who tend to fall by the wayside. By starting a Mercy Giver Ministry to reach out to them, these souls are more than likely to stay and grow in Christ.

B. Start a ministry to help battered women or children.
    The Mercy Givers of the congregation are great at this
    type of outreach. These are the type of Christians who
    will provide a kind ear to listen and who will reach out
    in love.

C. Take a foreign mission trip to a poor country.
    There are so many suffering people in poor countries
    around the world. Imagine the possibilities of a Mercy
    Giver taking care of hurting children in a village or
    ministering to dying saints at a hospital.

D. Start a letter-writing ministry to prisoners.
    Prison can be one of the loneliest places on earth and
    those incarcerated are often forgotten. Something as
    simple as a caring letter can make all the difference for
    not only the prisoner, but also for the Mercy Giver.

E. Spend time helping terminally-ill patients.
    The last moments of a person's life can be a very
    frightening time. Mercy Givers bring a great level of
    comfort to these individuals.

F. Make visits to nursing homes and hospitals.
    The majority of residents in a nursing home do not have
    regular visits. Mercy Givers can really make a huge
    difference in their lives by providing a loving heart, a
    compassionate ear, and meaningful interactions.

G. Volunteer in a pregnancy center for troubled teens.
    Imagine a scared teenage girl who just found out she is
    pregnant. Having a Mercy Giver available for them just
    might make all the difference in whether or not the
    innocent child is born.

Chapter Eleven

The Gift of Service

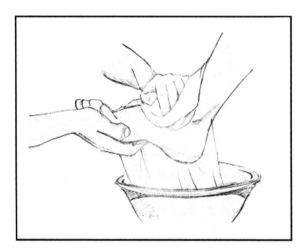

Service – The Passion of Helping (Romans 12:7; 1 Peter 4:10-11)

Romans 12:7, *"...if service, in his serving..."*

1 Peter 4:10-11, *"As each one has received a special gift, employ it in serving one another as good stewards of the manifold grace of God ... whoever serves is to do so as one who is serving by the strength which God supplies."*

Servants make up the largest category of Spiritual Giftedness, being about 21% of a typical congregation. The Greek word for service is diakonos, meaning "attendant or waiter." The simplest translation for the word is *servant*. There are three uses of the word in the New Testament.

1)   There is the office of the deacons in the church.
   • Timothy 3:12-13, *"Deacons must be husbands of only one wife, and good managers of their children and their own households. For those who have served well as deacons obtain for themselves a*

*high standing and great confidence in the faith
that is in Christ Jesus."*

- Philippians 1:1, *"To all the saints in Christ Jesus
who are in Philippi, including the overseers and
deacons."*
  [Note: These are leading male servants who have
  a wife and children. They manage the ministries of
  the church and are accountable to the eldership.]

2) There are specific ministries in the church.
    - 1 Corinthians 12:5, *"And there are varieties of
    ministries, and the same Lord."*

3) There are Servants in the church.
    - Romans 16:1, *"I commend to you our sister
    Phoebe, who is a servant of the church which is at
    Cenchrea."*

All three instances utilize the base word diakonos, but all
three are not the same in meaning. It is in the third example we
find the passion of the Servant. They are the individuals with
the ministerial passion of helping others. Since Servants are
typically the largest percentage of the Spiritual Gifts in a
congregation, they tend to provide outsiders with the first
impressions of the church family. They joyfully provide care
for others, being *maintenance people* for people. We all have
the obligation to serve, but Servants are compelled to work
harder, more diligently, and longer.

Nobody understood the servant concept better than Jesus.
Regard the words of Jesus in John 13:34, *"A new
commandment I give to you, that you love one another, even as
I have loved you, that you also love one another."* Do you
remember what Jesus was doing prior to this? That is right! He
was washing the disciples' feet. Normally this was the job of
a slave, but to Jesus it was the work of a true Servant! Mark

10:45 states, *"For even the Son of Man did not come to be served, but to serve, and to give His life a ransom for many."*

Those with the passion of Service deeply understand the "one another" concept in the New Testament. As one flaming Servant named Elizabeth in Iowa once told me, "My favorite passages in the Bible have always been the *one another* verses. I love it when people are helping each other!"

The soul with the Gift of Service focuses on the "one another" verses.

- Romans 12:10, *"Be devoted to one another in brotherly love; give preference to one another in honor."*
- Romans 13:8, *"Owe nothing to anyone except to love one another; for he who loves his neighbor has fulfilled the law."*
- Romans 14:19, *"So then let us pursue the things which make for peace and the building up of one another."*
- Galatians 5:13, *"For you were called to freedom, brethren; only do not turn your freedom into an opportunity for the flesh, but through love serve one another."*
- Hebrews 10:24, *"...and let us consider how to stimulate one another to love and good deeds..."*

Examples of Servants:
Anna

Luke mentioned in his gospel account of an early event in the life of Jesus. He spoke of a longtime widow named Anna in Luke 2:36-38. She was a faithful servant to God who *"...never left the temple, serving night and day with fastings and prayers."* We tend to view service as something of a physical nature, but for Anna it was also of a spiritual nature. Her service was defined through prayer and fasting. Through countless interviews I have found that Servants of the congregation tend to offer more prayers unto God than those of other Giftedness categories. Is it possible Servants view prayers offered for others as a service?

Martha

In Luke 10:38-42, we find an account of Jesus entering a certain village of Israel and being welcomed into the home of two sisters, Martha and Mary. Though they were siblings, the contrast of their Spiritual Gifts quickly became evident.

Jesus taught a lesson, and Mary *"was listening to the Lord's word, seated at His feet."* She appeared to have a passion of Teaching. She deeply desired to learn from the words which rolled off His tongue. Where was Martha at such a wonderful moment like this? Verse 40 states, *"But Martha was distracted with all her preparations..."* This is a classic signal that she has the ministerial passion of a Servant; they love to use their homes as tools to carry out their passion.

Does it end there? Nope. **Martha makes the common Spiritual Gifts mistake of trying to impose her passion on another.** She saw her sister and interrupted Jesus, demanding, *"Lord, do You not care that my sister has left me to do all the serving alone? **Then tell her to help me.**"* She was more worried about meal preparations than of deepening her knowledge of God's word. She expected Mary to have the same interest about her personal gift of Service.

What was Jesus's response? *"Martha, Martha, you are worried and bothered about so many things; but only a few things are necessary, really {only} one, for Mary has chosen the good part, which shall not be taken away from her."* You have to appreciate the patient and kind tone Jesus used with her. *"Martha, Martha!"*

How many times have we tried to impose our gift on someone else and overlooked Jesus's rebuke? *"Doug, Doug!"* How much damage have we inflicted on the church body over the years through this stifling of the God-given potential? *"Church, Church!"* Martha was worried about hot wings and nachos, but Mary wanted the meat of the scripture. Who was right with their passion, Martha or Mary? The answer is "Yes." They were equally passionate, but found themselves to be in conflict.

Signs of Maturity
1) They are *Creative.*
   A) They usually work well with their hands.
   B) They usually are resourceful with their means.
   C) They usually are good at meeting needs.

The mature Servant is a master of handiwork, for they have had so much practice. They are resourceful, making them more productive in ministering to people. They are good at meeting needs, seeing the purpose of their deeds. They relate to the words from the Scripture, *"Well done you good and faithful servant"* (Matthew 25:21 KJV).

The Passion of Jana
Back in December 1989, the dictatorship of Nicolae Ceausescu ended in a bloody revolution, and the deplorable conditions of the Romanian people were seen by the world. One of the greatest atrocities concerned the orphans of the nation. In the fall of 1990, ABC's *20/20* had an undercover special on the disgraceful conditions of the orphanages. It shook my Servant/Encourager wife to the core.

We were newly married and had already established a routine. Jana was a stay-at-home mom, and I worked until about 10 pm. She watched and recorded the program for me to view upon my return. Because Jana was a massive Servant, she always had a bowl of popcorn waiting for when I came through the door (I loved how she cared for me). That night I arrived: there was no Jana, no popcorn, and no greeting.

I thought she was occupied with the baby and lost track of time. All of a sudden she ran out of the room with tears streaming down her face, saying, "It was horrible!" I immediately thought something terrible had happened to our daughter.

Her emotional state was in response to the television special on the Romanian orphanages. The conditions were so awful that she had to leave the room multiple times just to pray and weep for the children. We watched the program together. The circumstances were ghastly. The orphans were in straight-jackets and stacked like loaves of bread on shelves. They were being beaten and thrown into corners like objects, completely disregarding the fact they had souls.

Being Evangelist, Teacher, and Prophet, I became furious at such a sight, saying, "Someone needs to punish them!" Jana reacted differently. Her passion again forced her out of the room numerous times to pray. She wanted to come to their aid spiritually and emotionally, but there was nothing else to do.

Throughout the hour, my perspective changed. I can honestly say it was the best look at her Spiritual Giftedness I have experienced. After it was over, I pledged that if there was ever an opportunity in the future to go serve the Romanian orphans, then we would take it.

Nine years passed, but the passion Jana shared with me still burned. In October of 1999, a friend, Ray Kesler, asked me if I would like to join him for a mission trip to Romania. I really wanted to, but it would have been over the Christmas break. To be away from my family during that time would have been a first and required the full blessing of Jana. I came home and informed her of the opportunity. Her concern had not dissipated over the years; she gave me the go-ahead.

While in Romania we visited one of the orphanages, distributed some funds, taught classes, and aided the poor. Arriving home, I shared the stories and photos with her and the kids. She was extremely pleased.

There would be other mission trips to Romania in the years to come. While there, we refurbished a wing of the hospital where orphans with AIDS went to die. It was a rewarding work that all started in the heart of an Encourager/Servant named Jana.

2) <u>They are incredibly *Spiritual.*</u>
   A) They generally pray more.
   B) They generally fellowship more.
   C) They generally are more patient.

Prayer to the mature Servant is not a chore, but a service. I have found they tend to pray fervently in meeting the needs of the saints. Since they are *maintenance people for people*, fellowship is second nature. Often the last people in the church building are the Servants, for they consider fellowship as part of their upkeep for others in the congregation. Mature Servants are also a patient group and are willing to make long-term investments of time in others.

The Uncrippled Passion

While holding a seminar in the Midwest and administering the written Spiritual Giftedness test to the congregation, I ran into an interesting situation. A middle-aged woman in a wheelchair came to me and questioned the results. The Multiple Sclerosis she suffered had crippled her whole body. She said, "I took the test and came back lowest in the Servant category, but truly believe I am a Servant according to the other four testing methods. How is this happening?"

I looked at the paper and asked her the first question, "I willingly do a variety of odd jobs to practically meet the needs of others." She answered, "I would *if I could*, but my condition does not allow me to."

Only then did I realize what happened. She did not answer the questions from the perspective of the *passion in her heart*, but with the *ability of the flesh*. My response in her case was to put before each statement, "if I could." When she answered the questions in that way, she was correct in her assertion, testing maximum in Servant.

I took some time to interview her in order to see how she was utilizing her passion from a wheelchair. She simply said, "There is nothing I can do, for I am crippled. I can't even clean my own home." I believe Jesus allows trials to enter our lives to make

the best of them. For her, she had a passion, but was unable to exercise it. What a heartbreaking dilemma to have!
I noticed her husband tested rather low in the same category.

With that information a proposal was brought forth. I explained to him that there are many activities in which his wife would have joy but she was not able to. I asked him to be her hands of service for the next month. "If she wants to do the dishes, then use your hands. If she says to wash them in a particular way, then use your hands to make it so. If she wants to move some boxes, then use your hands to do it the way she would have done it. If she wants to scrub the toilet and clean the bathroom, then use your hands to do it exactly the way she says."

What was the purpose of the exercise? It was two-fold. 1) She would be able to experience her passion through her husband's loving actions, causing a closeness which could be rewarding. 2) He would be able to experience her passion through guidance, causing a better understanding of what was in her heart. They did so and it brought great happiness, togetherness, and understanding of how the Spiritual Gifts work. I saw her a few months ago while traveling. She is more crippled than ever, but her *joy was full* and her husband's the same.

3) They have a strong work *Ethic.*
   A) They are thorough in their efforts.
   B) They are involved with anonymity.
   C) They are pleasant in their service.

Mature Servants are very thorough in their labors, knowing that it must be done right to be correct. They are not self-promoters, but anonymous in their work. When they carry out their labors, it is with joy on their faces. They have a work ethic which is second to none.

Jeanne the Servant Machine

There is a wonderful Christian woman in Pennsylvania named Jeanne. I first met her in 2002. What made her so awesome was her great passion of Service. For decades she has taken care of the flowers and plants at the church building. Her love for the work was evident in the final product, a well-groomed presentation of love in every flower bed.

Sometimes when the youth needed a ride to an event, she would be there, ready and willing to serve. On Wednesday nights, she hauled the trash out to the curb for pick up. If someone needed a visit at the hospital, she would go. Nobody told Jeanne to do those tasks, but she simply saw the need and moved to fill it. She sought no glory or trophy, but kept plugging away with joy.

Thirteen years later and now in her mid-seventies, crippled with arthritis and moving slower, Jeanne has not diminished in her Spiritual Gift of Service. On any given summer day, observers might see her in front of the church building, pulling weeds and digging in the dirt. Do not be fooled! The image is more than a gardener in the soil, but a classic example of a passionate Servant.

Signs of Immaturity
   1) They often *Fatigue.*
      A) They tend not to be able to say "NO."
      B) They tend to take on too much.
      C) They tend to take on impossible tasks.

When the person with the passion of Service is immature, bad situations can arise. They tend to not be able to say "No" when people ask them to do something. This leads to taking on too many tasks and the result is 'overload.' Their hardworking attitude is good, but with their inexperience, assessments of time requirements can be poor, causing them to be over-challenged.

The "Can't Say No" Servant
John was a very active Servant in the church family, but needed to mature in his passion. He enjoyed helping people

with any need, but had difficulty saying "No" to the many requests for help. Every now and then, there would be someone who tended to exploit this kindness by making unreasonable requests. They would ask for a ride and ended up making John their personal chauffeur. If they needed help on a project at their home, John became their carpenter. He simply allowed himself to be used by people who did not have Christ in mind.

At one point, some of these so-called "friends" took great advantage by having him drive across the country for a move. They were to pay him for the expense when they reached the destination, but they did not. They used John's car, his fuel and his time, not paying a dime. This really frustrated him and almost caused him give up on "people of faith." It was only through the encouragement of more mature Servants that he was able to learn not to be a doormat. He finally learned to say "No," when appropriate, and is now on a path of wiser service to God.

2)   They are led by *Emotions.*
    A) They tend to be over-talkative.
    B) They tend to be depressed.
    C) They tend to be too subjective.

Servants love to visit with others, but the immature must beware of becoming over-talkative. I have found this practice often leads to gossip and slander of others. They also are more susceptible to depression, finding it difficult to shift gears from activity to inactivity. When a novice Servant allows himself to be overworked and lacking proper rest, anxiety is a natural result. Another emotional weakness they likely will possess is being overly subjective in their analysis. They substitute activity in place of study and research, which never turns out well.

The Jealous Servant
Melissa was a Christian woman from a small church in Texas. Her Spiritual Gift was Servant, but her maturity level was low. She had been a practicing saint for many years, but in

her ministerial passion was an infant in Christ. Her primary ministry was heading up the church potluck meals. She not only brought a lot of food for the event but tried to control everyone involved. If someone attempted to assist in the church meals, they had to pass through "Guardian Melissa," lest they be rebuked.

Then along came Mary, the new sister who recently moved into the area and began attending the congregation. She was also a Servant and liked to help whenever possible. When the first monthly potluck occurred, Mary jumped right in to assist as she had in her last congregation. Melissa felt a bit territorial and even threatened, saying, "I have everything already taken care of."

A month later, Mary again wanted to help, but Melissa already planned everything in advance with some of the *potluck clique* group. Mary decided to step in and lend a hand anyway. Instead of viewing Mary as a comrade in Christ, Melissa expressed disapproval to her long-time girlfriends. They did not want new people intruding on their turf.

Of course Mary felt rejected and left out. It was not long before she sought a new spiritual home for ministerial employment. In the end, she found a congregation who really appreciated her desire to be plugged into the work of Christ. Thank God she found a church home that was a great fit!

3) They have personality *Struggles.*
   A) They tend to micromanage others.
   B) They tend to be indecisive.
   C) They tend to be overly passive.

A major weakness of the immature Servant is in their personality. Because they are driven by accomplishment in the area of service, they tend to micromanage others who do not share their passion. Others tend to be overwhelmed with their list of many things to do, leading to indecision and ultimately an overly-passive attitude. When life does not go as planned, the undeveloped Servant is easily thrown into polarity in decision-making.

The Single-Parent Servant

Jenny was a single parent mother of an eight-year-old son named Michael. The child's father was not in the picture, and she had a tough time raising him alone. Jenny was a fairly new Christian at that point in her life. She tried her best to bring up young Michael in the church family, but he proved to be a challenge. The greatest struggle she experienced was her immature Spiritual Gift of Service. This led to many problems which only complicated the issue of single parenthood.

It started out with her constantly caving to Michael's every need. To avoid an argument with him concerning the cleanliness of his room, she would end up cleaning it herself. When his messiness spread throughout the home, she expanded her own clean up as well. Jenny verbally chastened Michael about not doing the work, but in the end she would always do it herself. After all, her Servant heart really did not mind picking up after him.

Later on, when her son misbehaved in other areas, Jenny trained him to be *catered* to, literally. For example, she would call him to the table for supper and he wouldn't come because the video games were more interesting. Instead of missing out on supper, she would serve him the meal on the coffee table of the living room.

It wasn't long before Michael had become a spoiled, selfish brat. He had little respect for his doormat mother. He started back-talking, and she retaliated with micromanagement. He rebelled even more, and she pretty much gave up.

By the time Michael was in high school, he resolved not to come to church anymore. He was smoking pot, partying with his friends, and continuing to show disrespect for all authority figures. He hung out with the wrong people, did the wrong things, and went the wrong direction.

Where is Michael today? He is a resident in the state correctional facility. He picks up his room now because it is a prison cell. The guards are his new mother. Would it have been different if Jenny's ministerial passion was used properly? She struggles with that thought every day.

Some Ways to Obtain Joy with This Gift:

A) Make some meals and deliver them to others.
    It has been said that the way to a man's heart is through his stomach. The same is true for the Servant in reaching out to others with the love of Christ. Their meals are made with care and presented with joy.

B) Open your home for studies and meals.
    Servants are in their natural environment when at home. It is their greatest tool for the work of Christ. Opening the doors to their home will also open the doors to the hearts of the lost.

C) Be the first in line to assist someone in moving or some other undesirable job.
    Moving is a great stress. Why not start a welcome ministry for new families relocating to the area? Anything from unloading the moving van to painting a room will communicate your love for them.

D) Be a fix-it person for things in the church.
    There are many widows and single-parent mothers in congregations throughout the world. Imagine the joy they would feel knowing there is a repairman to lend a hand. A broken door, a leaking faucet, and routine maintenance for a vehicle might not seem like such a big deal to you, but to them it is an act of love.

E) Volunteer to be a chaperone at a youth function.
Often it is difficult to find chaperones for the
activities of a youth group. Don't wait for someone to
ask, but let them know that you would like to help in
that way.

F) Ask leaders for opportunities to serve, then follow-up.
The leaders in a congregation would be greatly
encouraged to know you are looking for tasks to help;
simply ask and go to work.

G) Work at a food bank.
Food banks can be a great ministry, but they need
Servants to keep shelves stocked, inventory itemized,
and food delivered to needy people. Partner with an
Administrator if possible, as it will make your job
much easier.

H) Share in the responsibilities of the church bulletin and
directories.
These are jobs that need to be done and require a
Servant heart. If you are from a large congregation
with a secretary, then offer to collect some materials
for the bulletin. If you are from a small congregation,
offer to do the bulletin yourself.

Chapter Twelve

The Gift of Administration

Administrator – The Passion of Management (Romans 12:8)

Romans 12:8, *"...he who leads, with diligence..."*

About 10% of a typical congregation has the ministerial passion of Administration. The Greek word Paul used for "leads" is proistemi (προΐ˙στημι), [pro "front" or "fore"] + [histemi "to stand or abide"]. The *New American Standard Hebrew-Aramaic and Greek Dictionaries: Updated Edition* defines it as "to put before, to set over, to rule." It is better translated from Paul's application in 1 Timothy chapter 3.

- Paul said in 1 Timothy 3:4 that an elder*"...must be one who manages* (ðñïß˙óôçìé) *his own household well, keeping his children under control with all dignity..."*

- He applied the same term in relation to deacons in 1
  Timothy 3:12, *"Deacons must be ... good managers*
  (ðñïß˙óôçìé) *of their children and their own
  households."*

Those with the Spiritual Gift of Administration stand before
others as leaders, hence they are *managers* among the people
of God. They embrace a longing to understand the immediate
and long-range goals of the work of Christ.

A captain of a ship filled with souls will chart a course
(Acts 27:11), finding safe passage through hidden reefs and
boisterous seas. He desires to safely guide his vessel, not just
for his protection, but for all on board. Administrators of the
church long to chart out a course of direction in search of the
safe harbor of heaven at the end of the journey. They are
visionaries and organizers, able to see the hidden flaws of a
plan which may shipwreck the faith of the members (1 Timothy
1:19).

Jethro, the father-in-law of Moses, demonstrated Administration.
In Exodus chapter 18, Moses was overwhelmed with the
responsibilities of a being the sole judge of Israel. Jethro, his
father-in-law, could see the strain it caused and decided to
intervene. He questioned Moses in verse 14, *"Why do you alone
sit as judge and all the people stand about you from morning
until evening?"* Perhaps his greater interest was how it might
affect his daughter and grandchildren. Maybe he was simply
being a good father-in-law. One thing for sure, he definitely
knew the flaws of the present path and offered a workable
solution.

Verses 17-19, 24, *"And Moses's father-in-law said to
him, 'The thing that you are doing is not good. You will
surely wear out, both yourself and these people who are*

with you, for the task is too heavy for you; you cannot do it alone. Now listen to me: I shall give you counsel, and God be with you...'.So Moses listened to his father-in-law, and did all that he had said."

His plan was to appoint godly, mature judges to whom he could delegate responsibilities. They would hear the cases and issue judgments. If there was a case which could not be judged at the lower courts, then it would be forwarded for Moses's discretion. Jethro's son-in-law listened because it was a good plan to adopt.

If a person wanted to build a house, they would call an architect. If a person desired better health, they would consult with a physical trainer. If the church of God, *the house of the Living God* (1 Timothy 3:15 KJV), expects to have sound health, they should utilize the guidance of those who possess the drive of an Administrator!

Gamaliel demonstrated this Gift.

In Acts chapter 5, the Jewish leaders attempted to purge the culture of Christianity. Their mechanism was through persecution of the church, beginning with the apostles. Defiantly, the apostles held steadfast, and the leaders desired to execute them in retaliation.

In the midst of the chaos, an old man named Gamaliel, a teacher of the Law, intervened. He pointed out the futility of their plan by saying the following:

Acts 5:35-39, "*And he said to them, 'Men of Israel, take care what you propose to do with these men. For some time ago Theudas rose up, claiming to be somebody, and a group of about four hundred men joined up with him. But he was killed, and all who followed him were dispersed and came to nothing. After this man, Judas of Galilee rose up in the days of the census and drew away some people after him; he too perished, and all*

*those who followed him were scattered. So in the
present case, I say to you, stay away from these men
and let them alone, for if this plan or action is of men,
it will be overthrown; but if it is of God, you will not be
able to overthrow them; or else you may even be found
fighting against God. "'*

Gamaliel reasoned that if the apostles' teachings were from
man, then they would eventually be overthrown. However, if
their teachings were from God, then they could not be defeated,
for the fight would be against God Himself. His suggestion was
to ignore the apostles and let the issue possibly die a slow death
over time. One can see the respect held for this man by the
other leaders in their response, verse 40, *"And they took his
advice... "* The plans of an Administrator will often be accepted,
for they are sound and worthy of pursuit.

The Apostles demonstrated this Gift.

In Acts 6:1-7, the young church was threatened with crisis
from within. The Widow Ministry had a major flaw of
partiality. Preferential treatment was being given to the
Hebrew-born widows over the proselytes (gentile Christians).
This caused great stress among the people, and the church was
about to experience a split. This elevated the matter to apostolic
intervention.

Their plan was to appoint a group of men to oversee the
widow's ministry, appointing individuals who were proselytes,
not Hebrew-born. It would be their job to carry out the ministry
to of all widows. They possessed experience in both Jewish and
Greek societies, making them culturally sensitive to the
widows' needs.

Verse 5 states, *"And the statement found approval with the
whole congregation."* It was a brilliant plan, and the church
members recognized it. Instead of a split, the Word of the Lord

kept spreading (vs. 7) and the church family grew stronger as a result. Had the apostles not demonstrated good management in crisis, division would have resulted.

Signs of Maturity
   1) They are effective *Planners*.
      A) They are charters and statisticians.
      B) They are accurate in assessment.
      C) They are goal-orientated.

The mature Administrators of a congregation are the analytic specialists and consultants. They pay attention to the empirical evidence of matters. Through their research and experience, they can identify the strengths and weaknesses of a plan. Administrators have great comfort in knowing a strategy is first evaluated and then implemented.

Coming Out of the Administrator Closet
Dave was a member of a church family in the Midwest. Like many congregations without an eldership, they relied on a monthly meeting to handle the business of the assembly. Dave always made it a point to attend the business meetings, including the discussion of the previous session. A professional contractor provided artist renderings of some options for expansion, so there was much to discuss.

The congregation weighed all the choices but could not come to a consensus. All the options seemed to be rather expensive, yet something still had to be done to make room for the increased membership. They agreed to take it up once again the following month to hopefully make a decision.

Later that week, I was at Dave's home to follow up on the testing and analysis of the congregation's Spiritual Giftedness. He was confirmed through the written giftedness exam to have scored highest in the category of Administrator. Most members would not have thought of him as an organizer because he had camouflaged signals. Further confirmation proved him to be *closeted* in his gift. Closeted is the term used for someone who has an incredible passion, but has yet to engage it. I decided to draw it out of him with some proactive questioning.

I asked, "According to this test, you are a statistician and charter." He was a bit quiet, but his wife ratted him out, "You have no idea, Doug. Do you remember that building expansion meeting at the building a few days ago? When he came home that evening, he pulled out his notebook and started sketching his own plans. He was at it for hours."

I asked Dave, "Is this true?" He replied, "Yes. I just wanted to see what we could save if we did it ourselves." I requested to see the notebook and two minutes later, he set it before me. They were far better than what the architect put forth! He not only had better options for the project, but his plans would have saved the congregation tens of thousands of dollars in the process. They were brilliant!

Pressing Dave a little more, I asked, "Were you going to show these to the brethren at the church?" He sheepishly replied, "They probably would not be interested in it." I really encouraged him to do so, saying, "Allow them to decide."

In the next meeting, he did just that. They loved his plans and reached an easy consensus to move forward. The project was completed ahead of time and under budget. Later on they made another addition to the building. A couple of summers ago, I was passing through and worshipped with them. I saw the finished product and it was wonderful! The church family helped unleash his gift of Administration in the way God intends for it to be done.

Later on he carried his Spiritual Gift into a new position-the Chair of the Board of Supervisors for his county. He did a great job, and this led him even further to employ his passion. He started his own construction company, specializing in remodeling and refurbishing. When a person is engaged in his or her Spiritual Gift for Christ, it changes the whole person for the entire world to benefit.

2) Their pace is *Deliberate.*
   A) They desire promptness.
   B) They desire preparedness.
   C) They desire completeness.

When the person develops the gift of Management, it shows in the manner which they present themselves. Administrators love to arrive to worship ten minutes early. They get stressed out when their spouse or children are causing them to be late or to arrive at the last minute – especially if they are teaching! They want *decency and order* because that is how God operates in His kingdom (1 Corinthians 14:40). To show up late to a meeting, unprepared in presentation, or incomplete in the finished product is not an option for the Manager.

Administrator "Beta Waves"

Back in the summer of 2002, Jana and I made a decision to move to another region of the country for ministry. There were many congregations looking for a preacher, so it was not hard to find employment. The most difficult part was trying to make the best decision among all the choices. Being low on the Gift of Management, I was suffering from a headache. I was overwhelmed and a bit stressed.

We had a wonderful, well-developed Administrator named Tom in our congregation. He was always nicely dressed because of his choice of career, a Chief Executive Officer of a large company. This was an Administrator's dream job! I visited Tom to ask for some guidance on the process. He happily agreed to assist me in screening my choices of congregations. Once a week, I would meet with him to pour over the information. He would ask pertinent questions that I might have otherwise overlooked. There was great comfort in having him assist me in the process.

One of the phone interviews I had was with Brian Dowler from Camp Hill. It was obvious to me from our conversation that he was very high in Administration. The congregation sounded like a good fit, but I needed to know for sure. I told Brian about Brother Tom and how he was assisting me in the screening process. I asked if it would be okay for Tom to give him a call. He agreed and the next day they spoke.

[Note: Why did I do that? I wanted to put two extreme Administrators together, for they are the planners of a congregation. They spoke the same spiritual language and, combined, possessed all the information which I required to make a decision. Tom knew me and my work from the previous congregation. Brian interviewed me and knew what was needed for Camp Hill. Connecting them would be the perfect way to see if I would be a good fit.]

An hour later, Tom called me. He said, "Wow Doug, you were right about Brian. He is a HUGE Administrator. I felt the 'Beta Waves' over the phone." He told me their discussion revealed that I would be a very good match for them and vice-versa. Brian agreed as well. Three weeks later, my wife and I flew out to meet the Camp Hill eldership for an interview.

Under Brian's direction, the congregation prepared a weekend-long interview process. This procedure involved the entire fellowship in the evaluation and hiring process, from the youth group to the elders and senior-citizen members. Sermons were evaluated, questions were provided for teams to ask, and all candidates were thoroughly scrutinized. They did not leave such an important decision up to a "trial sermon and one hour visit with the elders." This minister evaluation process has since been printed and has been used by other congregations.

Thirteen years later, I am still at the same congregation. This happened because Spiritual Giftedness was matriculated into the equation through the strengths of two like-minded Administrators. Together they could see the big picture.

3) They want to *Participate.*
   A) They are leaders.
   B) They are organizers.
   C) They are problem solvers.

Mature Administrators do not have to tell others that he or she is a leader, for they are known by their fruit (Matthew 12:33). They have a proven track record of being cool under crisis. Well-developed Administrators conduct themselves in an organized way, from the words they speak and the schedules they keep. People turn to them when they have problems because they know good advice will surely follow.

Lindbergh, the Organizer of People

The first members of the church I recall speaking with were Lindy and Carol. I was seeking a spiritual family to house my new found faith. My search was for a church family who believed in the whole Word of God (Psalm 119:160). Making a checklist with thirty simple questions from the Scriptures, I proceeded to call all forty-one churches in the phone book. My plan was to survey their perspectives and hopefully find a spiritual refuge.

When I called the Kirkwood Avenue Church, it was Carol who answered the phone. I introduced myself and immediately began the phone assessment. About the fifth question into the questionnaire, she said, "Hold on and I'll get my husband, Lindy; he is an elder in the church and could better answer the questions for you."

A few seconds later, Lindy was on the line and I continued the inquiry. I found him to be very concise in his answers and very organized in speech. It says in 1 Peter 3:15 for us to be *"ready to make a defense to everyone who asks you to give an account for the hope that is in you."* That was my perception of Lindy. He came across in a structured and genuine fashion. By the end of the call, I realized something amazing. Just from reading the Bible, we agreed on all thirty answers. I had found a church home.

I believe that God puts various people in our lives for a reason. He put Lindy in my life to give me structure early on in my Christian walk. Though he was thirty-five years older and from a different region of the country, we became good friends. I went to him countless times when needing guidance. He would usually start his answers with the question, "Well, what does the Bible say about that?" His grounded perspective brought order out of the chaos, which often hindered me. It was Lindy who took me to the Soul Winning Workshop which eventually led me into the full-time ministry. It was on the eight-hour trip back from Tulsa that weekend that he encouraged me to pursue it.

I didn't know the term back then, but I do now. Lindy had the drive of Administration, and it changed my life forever. Like the pilot of a ship, he guided me past those hidden reefs of distraction and helped chart a course for the future of my faith.

Nearly three decades later, Lindy and Carol have entered their mid-eighties and are still sharp as tacks. I always make it a point to stop by when back in my home state. While there, I share my dreams and ambitions with both of them. They will be sorely missed when the Lord takes them home to glory.

Signs of Immaturity
    1)   They can often be *Abrasive.*
        A) They tend to be pushy.
        B) They tend to be insensitive.
        C) They tend to be know-it-alls.

An immature Administrator often pushes in the wrong direction, taking the congregation from organization to disorganization. If educated, they tend to think they know it all by their early twenties. That leaves them open to be *"...conceited and fall into the condemnation incurred by the devil."* (1 Timothy 3:6) They tend to be hurtful towards those who do not agree with their plans, treating other opinions as an offensive attack.

Prideful Mike

Mike was a young, well-educated member of a struggling congregation. He really liked to make a difference in the church family and was active in several ministries. But, he was extremely immature in his Gift of Administration. Sure, he was book smart and had the degrees on the wall to prove it. But, being in his twenties, he was a baby when it came to practical application.

For instance, he was heavily involved in benevolence for the church. Homeless drifters and scammers loved to flock to Mike. He could not discern who was truly in need and who was not. The benevolence budget more than tripled in the first year under his charge. He was falling for very simple scams which could have easily been avoided had he only known how to sniff them out. We are told to be wise stewards with our resources (Luke 12:42). Mike had inadvertently taken money from the truly needy by giving it to scam artists.

A few years later, he was regularly teaching in the assembly and occasionally preaching. That is a great thing! Young men need to be encouraged to do that, however, it had become a bad thing for him because it inflated his ego.

Being the chairmen of benevolence and an up-and-coming leader, the power went to his head. He began demanding more of the eldership, not showing them honor (1 Timothy 5:17). When they attempted to admonish, he began to undermine their leadership.

It is important to note that Mike did not go into benevolence with bad intentions. His attitude evolved over time and put him on the path of haughtiness. He frustrated the elders and the preacher. He wrote organized lists of demands and generated a small following in the congregation. Before it was over, the preacher left, the eldership dissolved, and the congregation split. It began as a desire to offer direction for a church family, but turned into division in the end. If you have this Spiritual Gift and are young, please be mindful of this danger!

 2) They are often *Perfectionists.*
    A) They tend to be overly-competitive.
    B) They tend to be over-planned.
    C) They tend to be overdriven.

One of the great downfalls of the adolescent Administrator is when they are overtaken by their passion. Let's be honest, many times God *"causes His sun to rise on the evil and the good, and sends rain on the righteous and the unrighteous"* (Matthew 5:45). Countless times God has blessed us above and beyond natural blessings. The world calls it lucky, but Christians refer to it as being abundantly blessed.

When a young Administrator tastes early success out of proportion to their input, they actually might believe their "brilliance" caused it to happen. They fail to see God's hand in the circumstances. If failure finally occurs, they double down through *hyper-planning*, attempting to repeat success. This makes them uncomfortable to those around them. They become *plan-driven* instead of *people-driven*. Whenever anyone forgets they are working with souls, they become a hindrance to the kingdom.

Fast Eddie
Ed was a brother in Christ who graduated from college and started his career in the mid-nineties. He was always intrigued with the stock market because his ministerial passion was Administrator. He was constantly running numbers and looking at stock charts. He planned to make it big through investments and had a "system." Ed did give generously to charity and

planned to do the same on any earnings. His motives were good, but his management skills lacked experience.

He started investing at a great time and the Lord blessed him. There was a period of about five years that nearly everything he invested in made money. He had more than $150,000 by the fall of 1999. Some of his friends started calling him "Fast Eddie" because of how quick he was accumulating wealth. His wife recommended they payoff the house, but he wanted to keep reinvesting. Everyone else was making good money as well, but that would soon come to an end.

When the Bull Market turned Bear and the Dotcom Bubble burst in 2000, all his strategies proved worthless. The market tumbled, but he planned to outsmart it by doubling down. He even took out a second mortgage on the home to further do so. Before it was over, he lost nearly three-quarters of what he had earned. Calculating paying off the second mortgage, he barely broke even.

This situation could have been avoided. If only a mature Administrator would have pulled him aside and taught him a few things about finance and investments. They still called him "Fast Eddie," but this time it was for how quickly his riches went away.

   3) <u>They have a problem with *Pride.*</u>
     A) They tend to be slow to admit mistakes.
     B) They tend to be overconfident.
     C) They tend to be self-centered.

The Administrator's immature passion becomes obvious when their plans hinge on their "invincibility" to make mistakes. All of us, no matter how good we think we are, can and will overlook something. When an Administrator takes on such an arrogant position, they tend to think someone else made the mistake. If pressed to reveal the futility of their overconfident plan, they simply do not take it well. They usually damage many loved ones in the path of their pride.

Leading Without Leading

This can happen to anyone, even preachers. Frank was a minister in a small congregation. He was hired immediately after finishing his university studies. The church assumed that all ministers were the same in gospel drive, but not Frank. He was, in reality, an undeveloped Administrator. He was never going to fit the mold they were expecting, for he equated Minister and Planner as synonymous.

Everything he learned from the college concerning ministry was theory, not practical. His degree was not in the Bible, but in Business Administration. He wanted to be a manager of the church, not a minister. That should have been a dead giveaway to the congregation, but they knew nothing of Spiritual Giftedness. He did not like to make hospital visits; he did not like to volunteer for youth activities; he did not like to teach Bible classes. His ambition was to be a leader, without actually leading. He liked the designation of Minister but not the responsibilities that came with the title.

Paul said in Philippians 3:17, *"Brethren, join in following my example, and observe those who walk according to the pattern you have in us."* What kind of example did Paul set? He taught Bible classes, ministered to the poor, corrected the unruly, trained future leaders, worked the mission fields, and was persecuted for his faith in Christ.

Evangelism for Frank was writing out a "Master Plan" about evangelism, and then giving it to the congregation to carry out. The church family attempted to encourage him in the right direction, but things turned sour. He pulled the immature Administrator card in response, saying, "I am trying to lead, but nobody wants to follow." He just did not get it. Eventually he was fired and permanently left the ministry. Hopefully, he will be back when he matures.

Some Ways to Obtain Joy with This Gift:

A) Be the one to volunteer to gather information for projects.

Sometimes there is information that needs to be collected for church projects. Starting a new curriculum, compiling a list of people who are willing to be involved with a project, planning the cost for an addition to the building, and making a budget are all tasks that require planning. The Administrator will be up to the challenge.

B) Teach a class on personal finance for Christians.

Administrators are usually good at managing money. One of the greatest ministries a congregation can offer their members and community is a class on fiscal responsibility. Not only would this type of education help individuals but the church as a whole. When people learn how to manage their finances, they tend to give more generously.

C) Make yourself available to others for problem solving.

There are many in the church who are incredibly low in this passion. They could use someone like you to help in their life plans.

D) Analyze test results for a Spiritual Gifts class.

Be the one who is willing to accumulate the data concerning the Spiritual Gift demographics. Administrators can provide guidance concerning in the implementation of the research, and when they are involved, the probability of success increases.

E) Organize an event.

There are many ministries that can benefit from the talents of a keen Administrator. Vacation Bible

Schools, Bible bowls, and food banks are all in need of good planning before they are enacted. If there are new ministries suggested by an eldership or group, have Administrators review the plans. They will be able to reveal the potential strengths and weaknesses.

F) Be involved in the budgeting or volunteer to be church treasurer.
I have found that some of the best treasurers for congregations tend to be Administrators. They are meticulous with record keeping and appreciate accountability. Though it can be a lot of tedious work, the Administrator will do it well.

G) Be a chairperson for various committees.
Many congregations do not have elders and deacons. When that is applicable, then committees are needed. Why not be a leader in that way?

Chapter Thirteen

The Gift of Benevolence

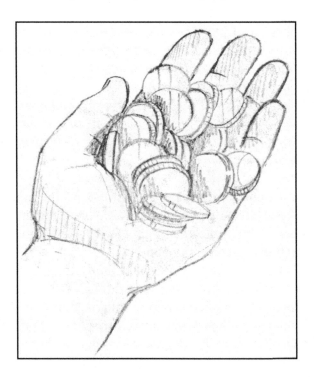

Gift of Giving –The Passion of Charity (Romans 12:8)
Romans 12:8, *"...he who gives, with liberality..."*

    The Givers make up about 2% of a typical congregation. The Greek word for "gives" means "to share." It refers to the ability to redistribute the blessings of God. In relation to the passion of Giving, it is the deep desire of needing to pass one's blessings to others who are in need. Some of the uses of this word are the following.

- Luke 3:11, *" And he would answer and say to them, 'Let the man who has two tunics <u>share</u> with him who has none; and let him who has food do likewise.'"*

- Ephesians 4:28, *"Let him who steals steal no longer; but rather let him labor, performing with his own hands what is good, in order that he may have {something} to share with him who has need."*
- 1Thessalonians 2:8, *"Having thus a fond affection for you, we were well-pleased to impart to you not only the gospel of God but also our own lives, because you had become very dear to us."*

We must not confuse regular charity with the ministerial passion of the Giver. The person with true passion in this gift does not ask, "How much can I give to the Lord?", but rather **"How much do I need to live on?"**

They are not concerned about daily bread, for they understand the perspective of giving through the eyes of God. It is this perspective which David summarized in Psalm 37:25, *"I have been young, and now I am old; yet I have not seen the righteous forsaken, or his descendants begging bread."* They strive to intensely understand the concept that God is the source of every spiritual blessing in Christ Jesus (Ephesians 1:3). He will *"...open for you the windows of heaven, and pour out for you a blessing until it overflows"* (Malachi 3:10). Their motto is "Give to God first and '...*all these things shall be added unto you'"* (Matthew 6:33).

To best understand the passion of the Giver, let us look at various examples of both generous and poor givers from the New Testament.

Examples of the Gift of Benevolence:
The Widow at the Treasury (Luke 21:1-4)

In Jesus' day, the Court of the Women in the Temple housed the treasury. It was lined with thirteen trumpet-shaped banks in which to make monetary offerings. The banks were called "trumpets" because they looked like trumpets. They were positioned with the broad side down and the narrow side facing up. People would load the coins from the top and it produced an echoed sound of falling coins.

In Luke 21:1-4, Jesus and the Apostles were at the temple treasury during the time of collection. Verse 1 states, *"And He looked up and saw the rich putting their gifts into the treasury."* To draw attention to themselves, some of the rich would be rather noisy when dropping their funds into the offering. Instead of giving a valuable gold coin, they might bring a large bag of the smaller coins in order to draw attention of others. Jesus condemned such practices in Matthew 6:2, *"So when you give to the poor, do not sound a trumpet before you, as the hypocrites do..."*

At that moment, the Lord peered through the group of people. He saw a widow make her offering. She was poor and greatly in need. According to verses 2-4, *"And He saw a poor widow putting in two small copper coins. And He said, 'Truly I say to you, this poor widow put in more than all of them; for they all out of their surplus put into the offering; but she out of her poverty put in all that she had to live on.'"*

It was not the amount she gave, nor the time chosen, but the attitude in which she carried it out. She had the heart of a Giver, having put in *"all that she had to live on."* She gave it all for the work of God. That put her in the position to be completely dependent on God for the rest.

The Macedonians

In 2 Corinthians 8:1-5, Paul used the Macedonians as a demonstration of the passion of Giving. *"Now, brethren, we {wish to} make known to you the grace of God which has been given in the churches of Macedonia, that in a great ordeal of affliction their abundance of joy and their deep poverty overflowed in the wealth of their liberality. For I testify that according to their ability, and beyond their ability {they gave} of their own accord, begging us with much entreaty for the favor of participation in the support of the saints, and {this,} not as we had expected, but they first gave themselves to the Lord and to us by the will of God."*

The Macedonian church was in extreme poverty, yet they gave *"beyond their ability"* towards mission work in Achaia. Being charitable in such a way placed them in a unique position. They gave in anticipation of God meeting their needs in the future. Paul held them up as an example for other congregations. 2 Corinthians 9:2 confirms this, *"...for I know your readiness, of which I boast about you to the Macedonians, namely, that Achaia has been prepared since last year, and your zeal has stirred up most of them."*

In Philippians 4:14-16, Paul wrote, *"Nevertheless, you have done well to share {with me} in my affliction. And you yourselves also know, Philippians, that at the first preaching of the gospel, after I departed from Macedonia, no church shared with me in the matter of giving and receiving but you alone; for even in Thessalonica you sent {a gift} more than once for my needs."* He was eternally grateful for their devotion to charity. Their spirit of giving enabled him in his drive for evangelism.

Bad Examples of Givers:
Ananias and Sapphira

Luke recorded in Acts 5:1-2, *"But a certain man named Ananias, with his wife Sapphira, sold a piece of property, and kept back {some} of the price for himself, with his wife's full knowledge, and bringing a portion of it, he laid it at the apostles' feet."* Ananias and his wife were pretending they possessed the passion of Benevolence. They likely recalled some church members who were strong in that Spiritual Gift, like Barnabas (Acts 4:36-37). They projected the appearance of being someone they were not, and it cost them dearly.

In the end, the two endeavored to trick the apostles, but were caught putting *"...the Spirit of the Lord to the test"* (Acts 5:9). They were unaware that the apostles had the miraculous gift of *"distinguishing of spirits"* (1 Corinthians 12:10), resulting in their deaths. We must not pretend to be someone when it comes to Spiritual Giftedness.

The Hypocrites

Jesus said in Matthew 6:2-4, *"When therefore you give alms, do not sound a trumpet before you, as the hypocrites do in the synagogues and in the streets, that they may be honored by men. Truly I say to you, they have their reward in full. But when you give alms, do not let your left hand know what your right hand is doing that your alms may be in secret; and your Father who sees in secret will repay you."*

The word rendered as *hypocrites* means "under the mask." It referred to an actor who had many masks and utilized them for entertainment. The audience never knew the real actor, for he was always camouflaged with the mask of another. Jesus called them *hypocrites* because they were wearing the face of a Giver, but in actuality were not charitable.

Signs of Maturity
    1)   They are *Generous.*
        A)   They give with liberality.
        B)   They give with wisdom.
        C)   They give with anonymity.

Being a mature Giver is something of remarkable beauty. It is often touted in the religious world that 10% is a good number to use for charitable giving. This is not always true for the one with the Spiritual Gift of Charity. Their giving percentage is often much higher on average. They view giving as a personal responsibility, not a chore. A mature Giver desires to be anonymous in their redistribution.

Benefactor Bob

Bob was always generous to the congregation where he attended. His favorite verse in the Bible from Jesus was found in Acts 20:25, for it is *"...more blessed to give than to receive."* He gave liberally to orphanages, colleges, mission workers, and evangelism. This was an early indication he had an extreme passion of Giving. Other clues were the following:

- When Bob would receive a paycheck, he would often pray over it before depositing.
- He would have his checks for the offering pre-written up to two months in advance. This was so he would be committed to his giving strategy.
- Before supporting a work, he did his research to make sure it was "Wise Steward" worthy.
- When funding a special project, he would often tell the treasurer to make sure it remained anonymous.

Luke 16:10 says, *"He who is faithful in a very little thing is faithful also in much; and he who is unrighteous in a very little thing is unrighteous also in much."* This passage teaches that if we are faithful in giving out of the little we have, then God will provide us more. This was very true for Bob. His company grew and so did his generosity. He funded many fine works in the brotherhood, and as a result, souls were saved and lives were changed.

Though he has gone on to be with the Lord, his influence is still felt today through a trust fund. Those things did not come about by accident, but through the ministerial passion of Giving.

2) They are *Charitable.*
   A) They are attentive to the needs of others.
   B) They are prayerful of the needs of others.
   C. They are committed to the needs of others.

Givers with maturity are very sensitive to the needs of the sufferers among them. Their screening process includes great prayer and consideration in regard to the Scriptures. This is positively compounded when there is a high Mercy Giver score alongside it.

The Heart-Felt Givers

Greg and Michelle were a lovely Christian couple I met many years ago at a Midwestern congregation. They were hard workers and good managers of their funds. They were, as it says in 1 Timothy 6:18, "*...generous and ready to share.*"

If there was a single parent of the congregation, struggling to make ends meet, they would secretly place an envelope of cash in their Bible. Sometimes they would simply give the funds directly to the church treasurer to pass on. They sought no personal glory, but simply wanted to glorify God.

For years, Greg and Michelle have been generous supporters of my works, funding orphanages, plane tickets, and various supplies. All of this has been carried out above and beyond their regular donation to the church. They could have purchased a bigger home and a nicer car, but instead they heavily invested in the kingdom of God. In return God has blessed them with the resources to continue their generosity.

2) They are *Reliable.*
    A) They tend to be lighthearted in crisis.
    B) They tend to be enduring in conflict.
    C) They tend to be dependable in poverty.

The Generous Giver from the Hut

We had just finished a hard day of preaching in some villages of southern India. Making the two-hour trip back to our place of residence, our guide mentioned that we would be stopping at the home of a Christian named Phalguni. Somewhere in between the banana and coconut groves, we came upon a small hut surrounded by a few water buffaloes. This was Phalguni's place of residence and we were his guests. He gave us hugs of appreciation and invited us to take a seat on his porch.

On the floor of the covered verandah was a wonderful banquet, complete with many vegetables, chapattis, curry chicken, and even items I did not recognize. It was a meal fit for a king! I was rather shocked to find such a spread in the middle of a remote location.

About halfway through the meal, our translator pulled me aside and shared a bit of pertinent information. Many months prior, Phalguni learned we were going to be in the region and begged to have us in his home. I mentioned to our guide that it was a very impressive meal. He whispered into my ear, "This brother spent about one month's wages to feed us today. He really has a generous heart."

His spirit of Benevolence was very sobering to me. We live in a nation that throws away more food than poor countries consume in a year. In my presence was a brother who pinched and saved for months to feed us. The smile on his face confirmed the complete satisfaction of a mature Giver. To him it was not really as much of a sacrifice as it was an honor. Before departing, we had a prayer together and hugged. I thanked God for utilizing his incredible passion of Giving.

Signs of Immaturity
    1)   They can have a bad *Attitude.*
        A)   They tend to be critical of lesser givers.
        B)   They tend to be critical of church budgets.
        C)   They tend to be self-critical.

When their gift is not developed, it can be a very sad situation. They tend to judge others through their own eyes instead of through Spiritual Giftedness. They will make an attempt to guilt others into giving which the Scripture clearly condemns (2 Corinthians 9:7). They feel guilty when the church family has money in the bank rather than on the mission field.

They also feel bad when their own finances will not permit abundant charity.

Critical Carol

Carol was a member of a congregation in the upper Midwest. She often made critical remarks concerning church budgets at the congregational business meetings. One of her statements made no sense at all to me. She said, "We should not even have any money in the bank because it indicates we do not trust in God." When the chairman countered her logic that funds were needed for future repairs to the building, emergency benevolence, and mission work, Carol dismissed it with disdain. She had the immature passion of Giving.

This became very apparent to me when she received her family's inheritance of $130,000. It wasn't long before the charlatans were beating down her door for handouts. She bought one person a used car; she bought a homeless man a trailer home; she bought groceries, food, and clothing for another person. She simply did not know how to say "No."

In one instance she brought a degenerate woman into her home to live for a short time. One week turned into many months, yet Carol deemed it cruel to kick her out. Throughout that time she paid for many of the woman's medical and physical needs. One night she called us at home and said she had been locked out of her own apartment by the woman!

At the end of one year Carol was out of money, jobless, homeless, and sleeping in her car. She ended up needing assistance from the congregation. How ironic that she went from being a critic of church budgets to needing to be a recipient of the same.

I asked her tough questions in the hope that she might learn from the experience. I inquired, "Carol, how many people came to Christ through your charitable giving?" Lowering her head in shame, she replied, "None of them." I encouraged her to be a wise steward of her blessings and to better screen the recipients of her charity. I have not heard from her in many years. I hope she matured the Spiritual Gift for God.

2)   They lack *Awareness.*
   A)   They tend to be unheard.
   B)   They tend to be underfunded.
   C)   They tend to be unprepared to receive.

Undeveloped Givers often demonstrate certain traits which hinder them. They usually fail to communicate their gift by being silent. Failing to develop the skills of money management, they are often underfunded. This disables their ability to give. Ironically, immature Givers do not like to receive charity themselves (possibly due to pride). It feels wrong to them because they prefer to be the one to give.

A Gypsy Named Minodora
   On my very first mission trip to Romania, I met a young gypsy named Robert. He was a member of a small congregation and also a student in my classes. Though not formally educated, he spoke English quite well and we spent much time together. He was my primary translator for the class on Spiritual Giftedness.
   The day before departing, Robert asked if I would pay a visit to his family. He said a few days prior, his four-year-old niece died from pneumonia and his family was in great grief. Naturally I agreed to make the stopover. We took a taxi across town to his home in the slums.
   When I came to the front door of the apartment complex, there was a stream of water trickling down the flight of steps. It had been warm that day. Some of the snow had melted and then leaked through the roof five stories above us. Entering their apartment, I was appalled at the conditions. It was a two-room dwelling with about five-hundred square feet of living space. Confined within lived Robert, his mother, a sister, her husband, and their three remaining children. There was a big

crack in the wall which allowed outdoor light and drafts to pass through. Their dwelling was rather chilly, which might have been a factor in the death of his niece.

It was there I met Robert's mother, Minodora. She was very gaunt with worn hands and a stressed face. She was holding her adult daughter, Gabriella; they had been weeping over the death of the young child. Robert introduced me and translated our conversation. They were not Christians.

For the next hour, I attempted to comfort them from the Scriptures. Apparently, the local Romanian Orthodox church would not allow them to hold the funeral in the church building because they were gypsies. They were told their child would not be in heaven because she had not been "sprinkled" with the infant baptism of the church! Naturally, this really upset them. I focused on the words of the Bible to debunk such a cruel and false doctrine. This appeared to console them.

About the time I was ready to leave, Minodora began to cry even more. Robert was speaking to her in Romanian; I could tell it was rather intense. Thinking she was still concerned over the death of her granddaughter, I asked him, "What does your mother not understand?" He responded, "That is not what we are now discussing." Pressing him further, "What is it then?" He softened his voice, saying, "My mother is grieved because she does not have anything to offer you."

I have never felt more humble and grateful for my own blessings. Living in utter poverty and losing a granddaughter to pneumonia was not her greatest grief for the moment, but rather that she could not offer me anything for my visit. She was a Giver/Servant and struggled with immaturity. I told her not to feel guilty about it. We informed her of our return trip the next year and she would have more time to prepare. I wanted her to know that she would be able to exercise her gift at that time. Her face lit up in anticipation.

Upon my return to Romania, I brought gifts from my home congregation for her and the family. I wanted to speak her language of the Giver. Entering the apartment, she gave me a warm hug and a kiss on my cheek. She offered me a handmade souvenir from her gypsy culture and we shared a meal. Most importantly she was open to a gospel presentation. Later that week, Minodora and Gabriella were both baptized into Christ. Her passion had taken her from great sadness of a dead granddaughter to the exhilarating joy of a life with Christ.

   3)   They can be *Gullible.*
        A)   They may not do their research.
        B)   They may give to unworthy causes.
        C)   They may be viewed as softies.

   Another indication that a Giver is immature concerns their gullibility. Instead of doing the research ahead of time, they are enamored with the act of giving. For this reason they are often viewed as pushovers. Left unresolved, it often leads to poor outcomes.

Duped Larry
   I knew of a brother named Larry, a member of the church in the Southern United States. For more than five years, he generously supported a Christian man from Africa, assisting him to go through medical school and become a medical doctor. For years Larry sent many thousands of dollars to pay for the expenses. Occasionally, the student sent letters of thanks and copies of his report card. Larry was very pleased with his investment, for he was an extreme Giver. The problem was he lacked maturity.
   In the fifth year of his support, Larry found a mission group that was traveling to that region of the world. He decided to surprise the student with a care package to be delivered by the missionaries. He looked forward to hearing about the happiness in the student's heart.
   When the mission group returned, they had very bad news. The student was not a doctor in training, but a dropout after

only 6 months. For nearly four years he took the funds under false pretenses. He was using the money to fund his immoral lifestyle, including prostitutes and drugs. To make matters worse, a simple Internet search revealed the student had received funds from two other supporters.

Larry was devastated for being duped into supporting such an effort. Instead of enabling a Christian for the works of the kingdom, he had empowered him for evil. He ended the support, learned his lesson, and matured. He still supports mission works, but now he always does the appropriate research in advance.

Some Ways to Obtain Joy with This Gift:

A) Organize and send surprise gifts to foreign missionaries.
   Missionaries can be greatly encouraged in receiving surprise care packages from the hand of Givers. The one with the gift of Charity receives a reward of being able to exercise his passion.

B) Support a student preacher through school.
   There are many in the brotherhood who would like to go to school for preaching and be better prepared for ministry. These individuals usually have to raise support in order to do this. If you have the passion of Giving and believe in the universal goal of reaching the lost, then support a preaching student. Call one of the schools and let them know you have such an interest. They will find a good candidate.

C) Sponsor a child.
   There are many charities in the brotherhood that minister to children. If one tests high in Giving and also Mercy Giver, consider this a viable option. Receiving letters from the children and knowing your charity made a difference will fill your heart with joy.

D) Secretly fund a needy brother or sister in Christ.
Go to the treasurer of your congregation and let him know of your intention to send funds to a needy member of the church. Doing it in that way not only makes the whole congregation look great, but also will satisfy the anonymity factor of the Giver.

E) Teach a class on the joys of giving.
Because they make up the lowest percentage in the Spiritual Gift categories, most people do not understand the joy of a true Giver. By allowing one with this gift to teach a class, the congregation will likely be much more giving in the future.

F) Be the presenter of charitable works in the church.
The typical pattern for benevolence in a congregation is the following: someone needs assistance, the elders or benevolence committee make a decision, a check is written out, and delivered. Why not allow the Givers of the congregation to be the ones to disperse it? They will have far more joy than someone who does not share the passion of Charity.

APPENDIX

Tests, Charts, Strategies and Congregational Report

Where Do We Go From Here?

I hope that what was covered in the last thirteen lessons will be more than just food for thought. This material is meant to empower you to make a difference in your life and in the lives of others. I pray you will embrace it on a congregational level as a platform to positively affect your community. That has been the intention from the beginning, and I hope you take up this challenge for the cause of Christ.

In this appendix, you will find some very helpful materials for testing yourself and the members of your congregation. You will know with a high rate of accuracy what your Spiritual Gifts are as well as the Giftedness profile of your congregation. There are also suggestions for implementation and development of strategy.

Lastly, there is a sample of a Congregational Feedback Report. This was generated for an eldership of a congregation which went through the course as a church family. These reports are provided for all churches who wish to hold a seminar for themselves.

If you have any questions, feel free to write me at CampHillPreacher@yahoo.com. I will respond to you at my earliest convenience. That leaves you with the question at the top of the page, *"Where do we go from here?"* That is up to you. May God bless you in your efforts to serve Him.

Doug Hamilton
Pulpit Minister and Evangelist
Camp Hill Church of Christ

Appendix for Spiritual Giftedness

A.   The Written Test   Page 223

B.   Charting of Spiritual Gifts   Page 228

C.   Common Questions   Page 229

D.   The Self-Analysis Test   Page 232

E.   The Third-Party Analysis Test   Page 233

F.   The Benefits of a Seminar   Page 234

G.   Sample Report of Congregaton   Page 235

Attachment A) The Personal Gift Assessment Test

Write the number that best describes your feelings in each statement.

-2: Never   -1: Rarely   0: Not sure   +1: Often +2: Always

1) _____ I am direct and persuasive in speaking to people about being wrong.
2) _____ I am not afraid to give advice to my peers.
3) _____ I love being the bearer of good news for others.
4) _____ When I am comfortable with a plan, then I move into action.
5) _____ I am ready to try the impossible because I know things will work out.
6) _____ I have the capacity to identify when something is wrong.
7) _____ It seems easy for me to learn difficult subjects.
8) _____ I identify with the forgotten of society.
9) _____ I am concerned about the comfort of others.
10) _____ I will do a variety of odd jobs to meet the needs of others.
11) _____ People with problems seem to come to me for advice.
12) _____ I adapt to cultures different from mine.
13) _____ I readily share information about my beliefs.
14) _____ I am emotionally hurt when people do wrong.
15) _____ I give money and possessions without expecting anything in return.
16) _____ I feel the need to make people feel welcome.
17) _____ Others tell me how much they appreciate my concern for them.
18) _____ I have a desire to help those who are suffering.
19) _____ I recognize the needs of others and immediately move to meet them.
20) _____ I feel compelled to smile when around others.

Appendix

Write the number that best describes your feelings in each statement.

-2: Never   -1: Rarely   0: Not sure   +1: Often   +2: Always

21) _____   People follow my leadership.

22) _____   I am a good manager of money.

23) _____   I feel a sense of adventure when traveling.

24) _____   I emotionally feel a need to help those in poverty, the physically sick or lonely.

25) _____   I enjoy evaluating results from studies and research.

26) _____   I look for ways to better communicate my thoughts.

27) _____   People say that I hold a positive outlook on life.

28) _____   People say they learn a lot when I teach.

29) _____   I gravitate towards the outcasts of society.

30) _____   I have no problem leaving possessions behind.

31) _____   I have a readiness to help if there is a job that needs to be done.

32) _____   People view me as impatient with others.

33) _____   I enjoy education and learning.

34) _____   I am concerned about making a good first impression.

35) _____   I am motivated by people more than tasks.

36) _____   It is hard for me to say "NO" when asked to help.

37) _____   I enjoy watching personal growth in individuals.

38) _____   I make difficult thoughts easy to understand.

39) _____   I enjoy delegating responsibilities to others.

40) _____   I double-check to make sure my facts are correct.

Write the number that best describes your feelings in each statement.

-2: Never   -1: Rarely   0: Not sure   +1: Often   +2: Always

41) _____ I feel compelled to expose the society's ills.

42) _____ People view me as being gentle.

43) _____ I feel the need to help when people are financially in need.

44) _____ I enjoy helping others who are in charge.

45) _____ I readily see the potential in others.

46) _____ Long-term relationships are important to me.

47) _____ I have a desire to know people from other cultures.

48) _____ I make people feel positive about themselves.

49) _____ I hurt when knowing others are in pain.

50) _____ I am not emotionally attached to my possessions.

51) _____ I make friends quickly.

52) _____ I readily take on obstacles of life.

53) _____ I am content to perform jobs that are considered unimportant by others.

54) _____ People value my answers to their questions.

55) _____ Taking responsibility for planning is not difficult for me.

56) _____ I feel the need to confront bad behavior.

57) _____ I am comfortable pressing people to make a decision.

58) _____ I willingly sacrifice to help others meet their needs.

59) _____ I desire to help when called upon.

60) _____ I build confidence in those who are unsure of themselves.

Appendix

Write the number that best describes your feelings in each statement.

-2: Never   -1: Rarely   0: Not sure   +1: Often   +2: Always

61) _____   I like working with my hands.

62) _____   I enjoy food from other cultures.

63) _____   I enjoy organizing people, ideas, and events.

64) _____   I seek to understand the emotional swings of those going through painful experiences.

65) _____   I know that things work out in the end.

66) _____   I believe that training is vital to improvement.

67) _____   I can tell when a person is lying to me.

68) _____   I enjoy giving anonymously.

69) _____   I enjoy working with facts and figures.

70) _____   Taking time for friends and family is extremely important.

71) _____   I am willing to learn whatever is necessary in order to help others.

72) _____   I tend to be the "life of the party."

73) _____   I become emotionally connected in other people's lives.

74) _____   I tend to take charge within groups.

75) _____   I feel the need to share my possessions.

76) _____   I have great joy in having people in my home.

77) _____   I am sensitive toward others who are in trouble or crisis.

78) _____   I easily learn other languages easily.

79) _____   I love to debate.

80) _____   I speak my opinion even when it is unpopular.

Instructions for Compiling Results

Add up the assigned points to the question numbers below. Record the totals in the right-hand column. After completing this step for all categories, record the highest three and the lowest two scores in the space provided below.

Administrator	4	25	39	45	55	63	69	74	_____
Encourager	9	16	20	27	35	48	60	77	_____
Evangelist	3	13	26	34	51	57	72	79	_____
Giver	15	22	43	50	58	65	68	75	_____
Shepherd	2	11	17	21	37	46	59	70	_____
Mercy Giver	8	18	24	29	42	49	64	73	_____
Missionary	5	12	23	30	47	52	62	78	_____
Prophet	1	6	14	32	41	56	67	80	_____
Servant	10	19	31	36	44	53	61	76	_____
Teacher	7	28	33	38	40	54	66	71	_____

Top three point totals:

Gift: _____   Points: _____

Gift: _____   Points: _____

Gift: _____   Points: _____

Lowest two point totals:

Gift: _____   Points: _____

Gift: _____   Points: _____

The #1 gift as revealed is very likely your primary gift. The next two are secondary and tertiary gifts. They are the means by which one will execute their primary passion to bring about fulfillment. For example, Barnabas, the Encourager, was known to use giving and teaching to encourage the brethren (Acts 4:36-37; 11:22-24).

Attachment B) Charting of Spiritual Gifts

Transfer the scores from the scoring sheet of the previous page. Circle the top three on the chart and underline the bottom two. In the event of a tie, use the information from the next page.

Tend to be subjective (more prayer and less study)

Prophet		Servant
Missionary		Mercy Giver

Generally exercised through speaking

Shepherd

Administrator

Generally exercised through service

Teacher		Encourager
Evangelist		Giver

Tend to be objective (more study and less prayer)

Top three point totals:

1) Gift: _____ Points: _____

2) Gift: _____ Points: _____

3)) Gift: _____ Points: _____

Lowest two point totals:

1) Gift: _____ Points: _____

2) Gift: _____ Points: _____

Attachment C) Common Questions

What if there is a tie in the top scores?

In the event that you experience a tie in the two or three top scores, then use the lowest scores to decide. This is because your highest score will typically be opposite of your lowest.

Take the example below. This particular individual tied for the highest in Evangelist and Prophet (12 pts. apiece). His lowest score was Encourager (-10). The most opposite of the two would be Prophet since it not only is on the other side, but also on the top. In this case the rating is #1 Prophet, #2 Evangelist and #3 Shepherd.

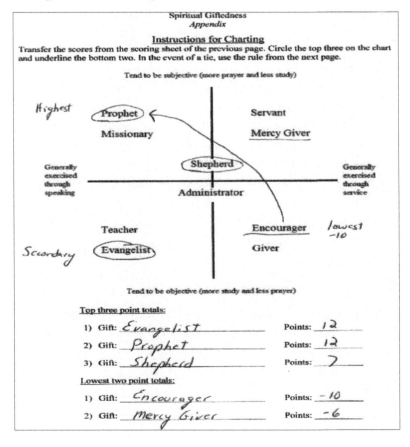

The other confirmations in the pages to come may also be used to further verify the data. The most important thing to remember is that this individual is not afraid to confront and is willing to share the gospel.

The same technique can be used in reverse for determining the lowest overall score in the case of a tie. Simply take the opposite of the highest.

In the very rare case that there is a tie on both the highs and lows, then use the data from the further tests. I have only had three people ever experience this situation. When they completed the Self-Analysis and the Third-Party Analysis, the Spiritual Gift became much more apparent.

What is the significance with the positive (+) and negative (-) values in the test?

The reason for using a positive (+) and negative (–) value is to gauge the present outlook of the individual taking the test. Of the many thousands who have taken it, I have found most register two-thirds positive and one-third in the negative value. Occasionally, someone will record all positive. This seems to point to a very positive outlook at the time of the test. Sometimes someone will test completely negative, indicating a negative outlook at the time of taking it. There are still high and low scores found within both cases.

[Special Note: Of those who tested negative on all Spiritual Gifts, a large majority did not stay faithful within the next two years. Is it possible that when someone does not hold a positive outlook that they are more at risk in the faith? Hebrews 3:13 states, *"But encourage one another day after day, as long as it is still called 'Today,' so that none of you will be hardened by the deceitfulness of sin."*]

The Clashing Couple

Years ago, a husband and wife took the tests home and administered them. Then they misplaced it in the house and were unable to find it. Two weeks later, they retook it and we recorded the results to analyze. They had about half positive and half negative results. Their results were split, half positive and half negative.

About two months later, they found the original tests and graded them. The scores were nearly identical, except for one difference. All of the scores on both tests were in the negative category. This was very intriguing to me.

I asked them what changed from the first testing to the second. They begrudgingly mentioned on the first they had a horrible fight and neither one of them were in any mood to take it. Then it dawned on me. All the rankings were the same, but all the scores turned negative. It was a reflection of their present outlook on life.

In retrospect, we must remain strong in our pursuits of obtaining joy in our Spiritual Giftedness. If we do, then there will be a natural immunity to many of the stresses of life which draw us into negativity.

Attachment D) The Spiritual Gifts Self-Analysis Sheet
     While studying each of the ten Christian passions, personally
rate yourself on a scale of 1 to 10. If one of the gifts describes you
very accurately, then give it a 9 or 10. If it does not describe you
at all, then rate it 1 or 2. If anything in between, then rank it
appropriately.

Administrator   _____

Encourager   _____

Evangelist   _____

Giver   _____

Shepherd   _____

Mercy Giver   _____

Missionary   _____

Prophet   _____

Servant   _____

Teacher   _____

Top three point totals:

Gift: _____   Points: _____

Gift: _____   Points: _____

Gift: _____   Points: _____

Lowest two point totals:

Gift: _____   Points: _____

Gift: _____   Points: _____

E) The Spiritual Gifts Third-Party Analysis Sheet

Provide this sheet to someone who knows you quite well. While studying each of the ten Christian passions, have them rate you on a scale of 1 to 10. If a particular gift really describes you, then give it a 9 or 10. If it does not describe you at all, then rate it 1 or 2. If they are fairly sure it is descriptive, then give it a 4-6.

Administrator   _____

Encourager   _____

Evangelist   _____

Giver   _____

Shepherd   _____

Mercy Giver   _____

Missionary   _____

Prophet   _____

Servant   _____

Teacher   _____

Top three point totals:

Gift: _____   Points: _____

Gift: _____   Points: _____

Gift: _____   Points: _____

Lowest two point totals:

Gift: _____   Points: _____

Gift: _____   Points: _____

Attachment F) The Benefits of a Seminar on Spiritual Giftedness

This publication and accompanying workbooks were assembled to incorporate Spiritual Giftedness in the local assembly over a thirteen-week quarter. This proves to be the best route for long-term results, for it engages the congregation in a healthy pattern of self-empowerment of their ministerial passions. They are more prone to carry the momentum from the initial process into regular ongoing analysis of newcomers, new converts, and the fainthearted.

This is not for everyone, for some congregations want to hold a Spiritual Giftedness Seminar. I have held these workshops for many congregations throughout the United States and overseas. The benefits of this method can be profitable for the churches that choose this path.

- It is typically carried out over the weekend through a series of seven lessons.

- There tends to be a higher participation rate from among the congregation.

- There is available ongoing interaction from the instructor for those who have further questions.

- At the end there is provided a detailed analysis and strategy sheet provided to the congregation (See attachment G).

Both options are viable choices for the congregation that is seeking to discover and employ their gifts. Most importantly, any fellowship seeking to grow spiritually in their relationship to God will benefit from this material, but only if it is employed.

Attachment G) Sample Report from Actual Congregation

The following is a sample report from an actual tested church family. The name of the congregation was retracted out of respect to autonomy and anonymity.

Church of Christ
Spiritual Giftedness Data

Prepared by Doug Hamilton
Camp Hill Church of Christ
3042 Cumberland Blvd.
Camp Hill, PA 17011
(717) 737-5587

Spiritual Giftedness
                    Appendix

Gifts Analysis for Church of Christ
According to the data collected from a large sample of the
congregation, the following assessment is offered.

Percentage Breakdown

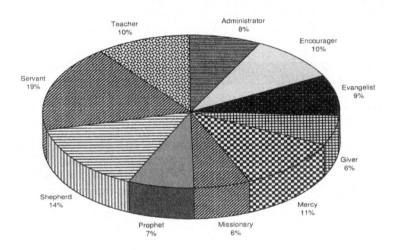

Strengths: Encourager, Teacher, Shepherd, and Prophet
    Your congregation is not afraid to reach out to others through
the means of their kind words and family environment, as
demonstrated by their high Encourager and Shepherd scores. The
people who would have a tendency to be attracted to this
congregation are looking for long-term relationships and a sense
of family, for they know they will find it here.
    Other lost souls who would be attracted to this church
family are those searching for a deep understanding of the
Word of God. Your high Teacher and Prophet scores indicate
that these individuals would find the congregation to be a
beacon of light for the truth of God's Word as well as being
willing to discipline when necessary, something that is
desperately needed in our society today.

The fact that your Evangelism passion is neither great nor small is not a detriment to your fruitful labors, for you will simply adjust as you empower your gifts from your strengths in other areas.

Weaknesses: Mercy Giver and Missionary
Your lower Missionary and Mercy Giver scores indicate that people may have a difficult time in the initial stages of getting to know you, particularly if they have different traditions, morals, or backgrounds. When combining this with your rather high Prophet scores, it can spell trouble if certain precautions are not taken. Your higher-than-normal Encourager scores seem to balance this out for now. If newcomers make it past the initial stages of acceptance, they will discover the congregation to be a warm, family-friendly group with purpose and meaning in their lives. If you remember to keep the focus on the important issues early on and strive to demonstrate your love for them, then it should not be a problem.

Another thing to be on the lookout for is the high Prophet with the low Mercy Giver mixture. This could spell trouble when not handled properly. Congregations that have this combination tend to over-correct and under-forgive in areas with struggling Christians. *2 Corinthians 2:7, "...so that on the contrary you should rather forgive and comfort {him} lest somehow such a one be overwhelmed by excessive sorrow."*

Overall:
In comparison to the average congregation, you have four primary fluctuations: Mercy Givers, Prophets, Givers, and Encouragers. The testing indicates that the assembly has 157% higher in Prophets, 51% higher in Encouragers, and 47% higher in Givers than the average tested group. On the other hand, you have 33% fewer Mercy Givers than average.

The remaining six gift distributions fall within the normal accepted averages; for the most part your church family is average. Taking into consideration the averages of all congregations who tested, and your strengths and weaknesses with the variances, the deviance chart reads as follows.

With the information on your congregation collected and understood, the following is a suggested strategy for the leadership of the assembly to consider.

Category	Average	Congregation	Deviation	Deviation Percentage
Teacher	8.8%	10.2%	1.4%	15.9%
Servant	20.8%	18.4%	-2.4%	-11.5%
Shepherd	14.4%	14.4%	0.0%	0.0%
Prophet	2.8%	7.2%	4.4%	157.1%
Missionary	5.7%	6.3%	0.6%	10.5%
Mercy Giver	16.6%	11.1%	-5.5%	-33.1%
Giver	4.2%	6.2%	2.0%	47.6%
Evangelist	9.2%	8.7%	-0.5%	-5.4%
Encourager	6.4%	9.7%	3.3%	51.6%
Administrator	9.5%	7.8%	-1.7%	-17.9%

We tend not to burn out when carrying out that for which we are passionate. It is also true that what we mentally dwell on will eventually work into our lives (Proverbs 23:7). Therefore it is important to labor in strengths, educate in weaknesses, and then incorporate together.

Here are a few suggestions to establish a pattern of behavior that follows this strategy. Your congregation received her lowest scores in Mercy Giving and Administration; therefore you should seek to educate in these areas. Your high scores were Prophet, Encourager, and Giver; therefore a strategy should reflect the following:

The intention of the chart is simply meant to generate a pattern of thought by the leadership. There are likely other ideas that would probably fit your situation, therefore do not try to limit the options.

✓**Labor in the Strengths** ✓**Educate in the Weaknesses** ✓**Slowly Combine the Two**	
Education	Labors
<u>Mercy Giving</u>: Have classes on suffering, understanding others, identifying society's hurting, Jesus his examples of mercy, dealing with sorrow, how to comfort those who have suffered death, <u>Administration</u>: Have classes on Leadership Development, The Eldership and Deacons, Leadership in the Community, and How Jesus Led.	<u>Prophet</u>: Confrontation ministry, prison mail ministry, rescue ministry, classes on how to keep sin out of our lives and the effects of sins. <u>Encourager</u>: Card- writing or phone ministry, shut-in ministry, nursing home visitation and sings, teen pregnancy crisis line <u>Giver</u>: Offer a course on Money Management and Budgeting for the other member and community. Fund some special projects for outreach.

<u>In Closing:</u>

We must remember that it is Christ who adds souls to the church. Whatever "recipe" that He has put together concerning your congregation is in fact *exactly* what will work for the furtherance of the kingdom in your area. Whenever a people seek to put Jesus first in their lives, the results will always be great. You are exactly what the Lord wants at this time and in this place (Esther 4:14). Make sure to follow your passions in Christ!

Your Fellow Servant,
Doug Hamilton

CPSIA information can be obtained
at www.ICGtesting.com
Printed in the USA
FSOW04n0532080715
8617FS